SLIGHTLY TO THE RIGHT

written and illustrated by
H. L. "BILL" RICHARDSON

CONSTRUCTIVE ACTION, INC.
P. O. BOX 4006
Whittier, California 90607

SLIGHTLY TO THE RIGHT

CONSTRUCTIVE ACTION, INC.
P. O. BOX 4006
Whittier, California 90607

Printed in the United States of America

I dislike political extremes, whether it be a total dictatorial state such as Communism, Fascism, Socialism or their political opposite, anarchy.

I like a Constitutional system such as ours, which is in the middle of the political spectrum . . . or maybe just

slightly to the right.

TABLE OF CONTENTS

DEDICATION

If you think this book is going to be a literary masterpiece, then forget it. I am a product of the progressive, permissive, regressive school of education (degenerate Deweyism), which has permeated the American scene for the past thirty years. My spelling is atrocious and my handwriting is a scribble, and if it weren't for the patience and fortitude of my volunteer secretaries and my captive wife, who for some unaccountable reason either escaped or rose above scholastic pablum, this book wouldn't be here today.

INTRODUCTION

Quite a few years ago on a hot summer afternoon, my back was literally against a wall. I was trying to disengage myself from an argument with one of my "left-wing" friends in the advertising business. I had stated that I was pretty upset with the international situation in general and our foreign policy in particular.

Before I could say another word, I found my friend putting me in the position of being against almost everything and everybody, including baseball, apple pie, and mom. To clarify the score, I love apple pie, used to play a pretty hot shortstop, and who doesn't like his mother?

But to hear my friends tell it, I was "against" and not "for"; I didn't care about the downtrodden and I was a warmonger who wanted to see America plunged into nuclear conflict and wanted the under-privileged to starve to death.

It wasn't long before I started to feel my ears tingle as the blood angrily rushed to my head . . . . my tongue was incoherently wagging in desperate defense, and I had the uncontrollable urge to smack him right in his smirking, smiling, collectivist coun-tenance. At this moment, sensing my impending overt, frustrated rage, he decided that the debate would soon turn into physical combat, so he dis-missed himself from my presence with a wave of his hand and a scurrilous parting shot of: "Oh, well, it's all relative anyway!" . . . . Gad, was I mad.

Later, in my car driving home, I was still mentally smarting from the debate. I had a deep sense of frustration because I darn well cared about hungry people, didn't like war, and resented being pushed into this position of being against everything. What made matters worse, this wasn't the first time, but it certainly was the worst going-over to which I had been subjected.

Why? I asked myself that question time and time again. I knew my facts, so why did I always find myself on the defensive? I then started, for the first time, to observe other such debates more analytically and began to notice some simple and all too obvious techniques that the collectivists have been using on me for years. I started to employ these techniques as I became aware of them, and all of a sudden I started winning arguments with the very same people who had used me as their prime target for verbal "kicks." In fact, after a while I even started converting some of them.

What I will be discussing in this book will not be a classical debate system under the Marquis of Ar-guesbury rules where each person has five minutes to state his views, and then the rebuttal, but the kind of conversational weapons you need in everyday discussions where you hope to convince your friends that our nation is in serious trouble.

Undoubtedly you have found that knowing your facts and proving your point with documentation doesn't necessarily guarantee a sale. How you present your position and your understanding of the person to whom you are speaking is almost as important as your information. Ask yourself, "How many times have I been irrefutably right on a matter and yet unable to convince the other person?"

One thing I hope this book will do is shed a little light on how you can better communicate with your friends who are less informed than you on the subjects of socialism, communism and welfare-statism.

If you are tired of being "shot down" in arguments by your "slightly to the left" friends, this book will give you guide-lines on how to win these discussions and, at the same time, not lose your friends. In fact, you might make converts out of them.

Sound impossible? Not at all. If you are willing to take a little criticism objectively and read this book with the thought of gaining knowledge instead of receiving an emotional kick, then practice what you learn; you can improve your ability to communicate. Tired of talking to yourself? Then do something about it!

(All references are listed on page 122)

CHAPTER I

GOOD GUYS ALWAYS WIN?

November 4, 1964. The sun shone brightly over Southern California, but over the more than one hundred "Goldwater for President" headquarters hung little clouds of gloom, easily seen by the discerning. It reminded me of that character in "Little

Abner" who has a storm cloud over his head wherever he goes.

What happened? For the first time since we-couldn't-remember-when, we had everything going for us. We had workers in the precincts, poll watchers, victory squads, and all the paraphernalia necessary for victory. We had a candidate who was a straight shooter (not from the hip, that is), or, as the Indians would say, a man who didn't speak with a forked tongue; a man of principle and proven integrity, and to top it all off, he was good-looking. We had facts and figures coming out of our ears, educational material by the boat-load, enthusiasm, boola-boola, not to mention zis-boom-bah.

The opposition was ideal. The candidate for President had been on both sides of the issues so often that it was unbelievable. His past record was so up-and-down that he was referred to as Yo-yo Bird. His running mate was even more unbelievable. His public record as an avowed southpaw could leave no doubts in anybody's mind. In fact, those who didn't believe it had only to ask him and he would proudly boast of it. His long public record of promoting socialism and "big daddy" government was common knowledge, and his praises were constantly being sung by contraltos of the Norman Thomas school of socialistic songbirds.

So, in all good conscience, we put two and two together and figured we had a winner. We felt it in our bones. "Good guys always win." We were conscious of a general public awareness of all these factors (so we thought). We certainly had taken the message into the precincts. We felt that the American people were capable of rational thought and if presented with a "Choice, Not an Echo," a choice would be made.

We could justifiably prove that this was not a matter of partisan politics . . . . in fact, it was and still is a matter of national survival. The issues crossed over political boundaries into the arena of what was best for our beloved America.

So, with verve and rugged tenacity, we threw ourselves into the fray, confident that Americans of all political beliefs would rally around the flag: "Onward, upward, straight shooters," "Don't give up the ship," "Morality forever," "Better dead than red," "Over the top, boys," . . . . you name it, we said it, and meant it too.

Late in the evening about midnight of November 3, we sat all huddled around the "boob tube" watching the results come pouring in. We were by that time in a state of suspended shock. We watched the "objective" commentators gleefully reporting the vote tally, savoring every new result before they shared the "glad tidings" with us.

After a while, I couldn't take it any more, so I gravitated into the kitchen to pour myself a drink. For a moment I considered Hemlock on the rocks or Arsenic and tonic with a twist, but finally decided on a milder concoction. I found a sour mash made in one of the states that went for Goldwater and poured myself a healthy one. I am not a drinking man, by and large, but that night it wouldn't have made any difference anyway. I was so numb that I doubt if even the Hemlock on the rocks would have affected me.

The doorbell rang; other friends started to arrive at our home for the wake. Before long a large number of gloomy-faced friends had gathered in the den, and, in typical fashion, we started to contemplate what went wrong . . . . what should we do, form a suicide pact, ride the decline, or fight again?

The comments came fast and heavy. Strong opinions mark informed people, and they are almost never hesitant in stating them.

"What's *wrong* with people, can't they SEE what's happening?"

"Boy, are we in for it!"

"They DESERVE slavery!"

"Pass the tonic!"

"Why are people so *dumb* . . . . couldn't they see the difference?"

"Aw . . . . they just don't care!"

"*Everybody* wants a handout."

"I'm *disgusted* with people."

"Where's the ice?"

"It's just like Rome in the last years . . . . we're on the decline."

"Everybody's been *brainwashed!*"

"Gee, I *thought* I had my precinct."

It went on into the wee hours. In the background the constant drone of the television reported the ever-increasing size of the defeat; now and then a congressional race was reported with the same devastating results.

We had been soundly defeated. Why?

CHAPTER II

INSPECT YOURSELF!

There's an old political axiom that "you learn more from your defeats than your victories." In many ways this is true, but this expression certainly cannot be categorized as a truism.

Conservatives have been losing elections and discussions for years and the "Liberals" have been winning. You would think that we would learn from our past defeats and win for a change, but unfortunately that hasn't been the case. By this time if "learning from past defeats" were true, we should be mental giants.

There is another old expression which is much more apropos: "A fox always smells his own burrow first." In other words, before we start blaming everybody else, let's look at ourselves.

First, Conservatives are LOUSY communicators. Sometimes I think we would have trouble selling whale blubber to a rich starving Eskimo. Because of our basic nature, we think that all we have to do is speak the truth and the sale is made. We are constantly being shocked out of our shoes by friends who not only reject what we say, but look upon us as a group of squirrels gathering nuts. Many of us are as welcome in social gatherings as the bubonic plague. I can speak from a position of authority because of my past experiences. There was a time when I would go to a cocktail party, walk into the house and stare at an empty room. I swear people would evaporate into the woodwork to avoid me. They stopped asking: "What's new, Bill?" because I would, in no uncertain terms, tell them. It took years before I had the sense to ask myself, "Say, maybe I'm approaching this all wrong." I had been practicing conservative dialectics, one step forward, two back.

Introspection is a difficult task. It is difficult to admit mistakes once you find them, and *very* difficult to correct them. For myself it's been a painful process, but the pain is more than offset by the gain from this self-inspection.

I am now a more effective salesman for my beliefs. My friends no longer turn into ectoplasm and evaporate before my eyes when I open my mouth. I am being invited back to parties, and people are even asking my opinion on matters concerning our country. It's a jim-dandy feeling.

How did I become a more effective conversationalist? Well, that's what this book is all about. If I could condense it into a single paragraph, I would put it on a record and get rich. Let's look at the many reasons why we are not effective communicators. Let's investigate, one by one, the goofs we make, and then explore some of the effective tools our dedicated opposition uses.

What is communication? Communication is the

ability to impart information in such a manner that it is understood and remembered. Talking to somebody isn't necessarily communicating. We have all talked to people, but talking obviously hasn't been enough. Unfortunately, the other person has to listen. If talking were enough, we would have won long ago. The tongue is a two-edged sword. You can talk people into believing you or, through what you say (and how you say it), you can drive people away.

What does communication mean to our enemies? A great deal. In fact, through their ability to communicate ideas and disguise their programs, and by controlling certain facets of the communications media, they have been attempting to lead this country down the road to socialism. The fantastic amount of attention that the Communists and Socialists give to the propaganda media should make all of us wonder . . . . why do they give it such importance? Let's briefly investigate what communication means to them and what effect they wish it to have upon us.

CHAPTER III

CONTROLLED COMMUNICATIONS

Deception and guile are tactics that have been used since the devil induced Eve to stick an apple under Adam's nose. Unfortunately, people have been biting on Satan's fruit ever since. Down through history devious men have used trickery as a tool of war. The Trojans with their horse outside the gates yelling, "There ain't nobody here but us cowboys" to our State Department with their, "There ain't nobody here but us Liberals."

In the past, propaganda was used with hit-and-miss effectiveness. Today, the dissemination of controlled propaganda is a cold, calculated, mathematical science analytically tested and retested. Now it is a studied art, a central and dominant factor of world conquest.

To ignore the strategic use of propaganda as an effective tool of war is to literally commit national suicide. To believe that you, the reader, have not in one way or another been affected by this science, is the height of gullibility. We all have been affected by it, Conservative and Liberal alike.

It would be impossible in one book to go into all the facets of propaganda and psychological warfare because of the broadness of the subject, but it is important that we briefly touch upon one phase . . . . Cybernetic Warfare.

The word "Cybernetics" is derived from the Greek "Kybernētikē," which means the art of steersmanship. In other words, to steer or control. To Communists, Cybernetics means to control or steer communications in such a manner as to achieve specific results in promoting their world power grab.

Cybernetics is the science of giving controlled doses of propaganda to a broad sector of the population without their knowledge. The intention is to condition Americans to react in a given manner at a given signal.

The conspiracy, through a long, slow process of patient infiltration, is laying the foundation for manipulation of the information most Americans receive. If you were conspirators and wanted to take over our country, wouldn't the manipulation of communications be an important factor?

Where did the Communists get the idea in the first place of controlling people through this form of brainwashing? Edward Hunter, probably the world's foremost authority on brainwashing, stated, *"The basis for modern psychological warfare, which makes it different from whatever was done in the past, are the findings of the Russian physiologist, Pavlov. He was not a Communist. He had completed his most important discoveries before the Communists took power. His first discovery was the effectiveness of using a living animal in experiments, rather than a dead animal. His second great discovery was that the instincts of an animal, which we call reflexes, were of two kinds. One was the reflexes which the animal was born with, it's unconditioned reflexes. The other was its conditioned reflexes, which man can train into the animal. Most of us have heard of Pavlov's experiments with dogs and lights. He first provided a bowl of food and turned on a light of a certain color, then an empty bowl and turned on a different colored light. After he had done this a number of times, he turned on the light that accompanied the food, but presented an empty bowl to the animal, and the dog deposited just as much saliva as when the bowl was full. When he presented a bowl full of food with the wrong light, the animal did not eat."[1]*

By this time you are probably wondering what does a salivating mongrel have to do with me? Let's continue the quote and see.

"After he had switched the lights and the bowls of food, the dog became neurotic, barked, and was driven into a state which among human beings we call insanity.

"When the Communist hierarchy in Moscow discovered that it was unable to persuade people willingly to follow Communism, when they found they could not create what they wanted, the 'new Soviet man' in which human nature would be changed, they turned to Pavlov and his experiments. They considered people the same as animals anyway and refused to recognize the role of reason or divinity in the human being. They took over the Pavlovian experiments on animals and extended them to people. They did so with the objective of changing human nature and creating a 'new Soviet man.' People, they anticipated, would react voluntarily under Pavlovian pressures, in the way the dog does, to Communist orders, exactly as ants do in their collectivized society."[2]

The last sentence really gives us an insight into the Communist interest in communications. Instead of lights, as Pavlov used them to condition animals, Communists are using communications to condition us. It has been forty years since Pavlov's original experiments, and the Communists have progressed substantially since then in their refinement of this Pavlovian process. In other words, to take over a country that's stronger than yours, infiltrate and subvert the communications and educational processes of your enemy. Thus, over a sustained period of time, you gain control of the information he receives. When you have conditioned (educated) him sufficiently to react for, or against, whatever you choose, it is then just a matter of time until he is in your power.

Usually at this point someone will say: "Well, Jocko, that sounds great in theory, but it can't happen here. It's impossible to take over all of the communications in a country as large as America." In part, this is right. It would be practically impossible to take over ALL communications, but they don't need ALL, just the key positions.

Let me give a few examples of how it could work. Television Station PDQL has on its staff a typical group of Commentators, no dumber or brighter than any other sector of the professional community. Their news coverage has definitely given the impression of being extremely biased favoring "big daddy" government. It is natural to assume that the Commentators themselves MUST know what they are doing, but this isn't necessarily the case.

Every TV Station has a dispatch desk. The Dispatcher in Station PDQL sends the Reporters out to cover certain assignments that the Dispatcher deems newsworthy. In this particular station the Dispatcher, more than 80% of the time, sends the Reporters to interview only those of strong left-wing persuasion. Over a period of years the Station's Commentators naturally become more and more indoctrinated and the viewing audience is led to the left.

Another example: Station RUCK has the same type

of Commentators and it too gives the definite left-wing slant all of the time. Only this time it's not the Dispatcher . . . . it's the Film Editor who is playing hanky panky with the scissors.

A Journeyman Reporter, with Camerman and Soundman, receives an assignment to interview a man who opposes the concept of "big daddy" government. The interview lasts five minutes. The man states his position clearly and accurately. The crew then departs to interview the other side of the argument and tapes again for five minutes. Now back to the studio. The Film Cutter scans the ten minutes of interviews, and happily goes to work with the scissors. The best of the first man's statements wind up on the cutting room floor, and the best of the leftist is seen by the viewing audience.

Another example: Let's say this time a dedicated leftist worms his way into a strategic information position within our government. Many of the legitimate newsmen depend upon reliable information from government officials to keep the public informed about our Nation's affairs. This leftist official takes it upon himself to "manage" news so that it won't embarrass his particular department.

On December 6, 1962, Arthur Sylvester, Assistant Secretary of Defense, stated, *"I think the inherent right of the government to lie . . . . to lie to save itself when faced with nuclear disaster . . . . is basic."*[3]

Mr. Willard Edwards, a respected Washington Correspondent, commenting on Sylvester's statement, said, *"There we had it. The government has both an inherent and basic right to falsify news in the name of self-preservation. . . ."*[4]

Mr. Edwards was shocked by such a statement. How about you?

Herb Philbrick served nine years in the Communist apparatus for the F.B.I. as a Counter Agent for our government. One of the segments of the Communist structure he worked within was the Agit-Prop (agitation-propaganda) division. Mr. Philbrick has repeatedly warned Americans to be aware of Communist effectiveness in communications.

All too often we think that the conspiracy spends all of its time telling lies. That's not necessarily true. You can be brainwashed to a certain viewpoint by what you DON'T hear almost as much as by what you DO hear. Omission is a strategic weapon and almost impossible to detect. If Americans could accurately see both sides of the question, communism and socialism wouldn't be around today. If most Americans were even slightly aware of the brutality of communism, they wouldn't tolerate the present situation. But, unfortunately, most Americans don't comprehend the insidious nature of the beast. This general lack of knowledge of the conspiracy isn't accidental, it's planned.

In the above examples you have seen how just a few people properly placed, can effect fantastic control over communications. The Communists understand this all too well, and are constantly working toward this goal of total manipulation of communications. As the Communists have stated: "Comrade, one person in the right place at the right time is all we need."

In communications, as in any of our major institutions, a few properly placed can do fantastic damage. The Communists have no intention of showing their hand all at once. They have more patience than most red-blooded Americans. Slow gradualism always has been one of their methods. The degree and intensity of what the conspirators want us to hear through all the channels of communication is a key factor in their brainwashing of the public.

(See Appendix I for further details.)

CHAPTER IV

TRIGGER WORDS

We use words to communicate with each other. When we group words together in a well arranged order, they serve as a bridge of understanding between people. Words are important as long as their meanings remain consistent. If the meanings of all words were in a constant state of flux, the communication of ideas would be impossible. It once was stated that: "When man destroys his relationship to his words he destroys his touch with reality . . . ."

Confusing the meaning of words is an age-old art. It is now a studied science, used by Communists to confuse large segments of the world population, while at the same time relaying specific instructions to the party faithful. They refer to it as Aesopian or "sectarian" Language. It is quite simply . . . . semantic weaponry.

Dr. Stefan T. Possony, a recognized authority on Communist semantic tricks, stated: *"Every Communist communication must convey an orthodox, that is, revolutionarily activating message to the party and its followers. This same communication must convey a different, i.e., soothing, pacifying, and paralyzing message to the opponent of communism."*[5]

Communists, have, over a period of years, ". . . cleaned up the language which they addressed to the noninitiated"[6] *. . . . change meanings of words, confuse, destroy their meanings, and through this semantic weaponry, condition people. ". . . . The Communist message should be couched in terms which have a positive ring in the ears of the audience. Communism must be dressed up as something like democratic liberalism or patriotic nationlism. Offensive and locally unfamiliar terms must be avoided . . . . any good Communist would now be able to use language which is not to be found in the classical writings of Marx and Lenin but occurs in Jefferson, Mill—or Jane Addams."*[7]

"Of course, Communist terminology could not be cleaned up entirely, but, briefly, "revolution" became "liberation," and the physical extermination of entire groups of people, "classes," and nations became the "laying of the foundations of socialism." Occasionally, even the word "communism" disappeared from the vocabulary and was replaced by "anti-fascism" or, more recently, "anti-imperialism . . . . Lenin, who invented, among Communists, those tactics of language, occasionally even abandoned the use of his favorite word, "revolution"; instead, he talked about the reform, which he contrasted to reforms."[8]

In conversations with friends who are not well informed on semantic chicanery, you will find you have to continually define words so that you both understand each other. This is especially true in any conversation that you might have on politics or communism. Many Americans have accepted new meanings of certain words and phrases which in the classic interpretation would be incorrect. As an example, let's take the word "conservative." The dictionary defines a political conservative as:

1. "A person tending to preserve from ruin or injury.
2. One who aims to preserve from innovation or radical change; one who wishes to maintain an institution or form of government in its present state."

From this definition you MIGHT call us Conservatives because we want to conserve the constitutional structure as it was intended, but we have no intention of conserving some of our present programs such as Foreign Aid to communist enemies, coexistence, and deficit spending. From the classical definition of the word, Adlai Stevenson would be a Conservative, because he and others of the same political persuasion are trying to conserve our present policies.

"Conservative" to present day Conservatives usually means one who loves his country and its institution, opposes totalitarianism, believes in individual freedom, is not selfish or bigoted, embraces other people's interests, and advocates greater freedom of thought and action. Don't get "shook," but I have just given you Webster's Dictionary's definition of "liberal." If you don't believe me, look it up.

"Conservatism" to Communists means one thing only . . . . active opposition, or as they call it, Fascism.

"Conservatism" to the laboring man generally gives rise to anti-labor thoughts.

"Conservatism" to the Socialist means opposition to a planned economy.

Always remember this . . . . NEVER ASSUME THAT
THE PERSON TO WHOM YOU ARE SPEAKING DEFINES
WORDS EXACTLY AS YOU DO, especially if he holds dif-
ferent political views.

We often assume people understand the terminology we use. If you are talking to a labor union
man who reads and believes only Union publications,
he could think Conservatives are death warmed
over, and if in a conversation with this man you
say, "I'm a Conservative and proud of it," and you
assume that he feels the same way about the word
"Conservative" as you do, you've made a grave mistake. He, in all probability, believes that YOU have
the same conception of the word "Conservative" that
HE does. In other words, he probably thinks, "Why
this So and So is anti-Labor and proud of it!!!"

Here are a few of the words that the Communists
use and their Communist definitions:

Fascist	An active, effective anti-Communist.
Right Winger	One who tends toward an anti-Communist government.
Co-existence	A temporary situation until the Communists gain time to infiltrate, subvert and gain strength.
Peace	The final victory over Capitalism.
Democracy	A one-world socialist state under Communism.
Emerging Nations	Nations that throw off Feudalism and gravitate towards Communism.
Neutral Nations	Pro-Soviet Nations.
Reforms	Programs that centralize controls and destroy Free Enterprise.
Progressive	Any pro-Soviet movement.

When a high Soviet official says with a big, fat

smile, "I'm for peace and democracy," .... Americans say, "Why, he isn't so bad, he's for the same thing I am."

Nonsense! In their Aesopian language he has stated emphatically, "I'm for winning this war and the final emergence of a one-world Communist State."

TRIGGER WORDS

Certain specific words are not only vehicles for transmitting information (when properly understood), but they are also triggers which evoke strong emotional reactions. As discussed in Chapter 3, emotions can be stored systematically within the mind. Stored emotions need words or graphic symbols to act as trigger mechanisms, which release these stored feelings. Words can and do trigger certain non-thinking emotional reactions.

The Communists build strong emotional feelings toward certain words. They then use these words as "scare symbols" to activate people in specified directions. Americans have strong emotional feelings toward certain American symbols, such as the word "Lincoln." The thought of Lincoln makes us think of honesty, integrity, fairness, love of country, strength, etc. In Chicago, many years ago, the Communists set up a school on Communism and called it the "Lincoln School," using the emotional impact of Lincoln's name to their advantage.

The word "American" has wonderful connotations to us all. Communists understand this well. A fantastic percentage of their communist fronts use the word "American" somewhere in the title.

Communists also like to build words into effective trigger weapons which bring about feelings of disgust. Extremism is one such word. Americans have an honest aversion toward political extremes, and rightly so. Our Nation is founded on balanced, rational thought. Whenever organized opposition toward communism arises, the Communists immediately try to falsely identify these organizations as "extreme," and if the Communists are effective, they emotionally chase people away from these patriotic organizations. They also do this to individuals.

Many times Communists know that in the future they will be opposed on certain programs that they haven't as yet implemented. They will build slogans and trigger words in advance, so that when the time comes people will react as desired.

For many years in this country the Communists used the word "McCarthyite" with great effectiveness. They took this manufactured word and built fantastic emotions around it. In the creation of the scare word, they systematically destroyed Joe McCarthy the man.

McCarthyism still holds many sad memories for me. When I was in college, I was affected by the unfavorable propaganda relating to Senator McCarthy. I was anti-Communist, but I swallowed hook, line and sinker, the anti-McCarthy propaganda. It wasn't until years later and after much research on the subject, that I recognized the disservice I had done this man. I still smart when I think about it.

New "trigger words" are constantly being thrown into the mental American hopper, and many old ones constantly revived . . . . to name a few: ultra-conservative, extremists, neo-Fascists, Goldwaterites, Birchite, anti-semite, etc.

One tactic that is a favorite of the Communists is to take their strongest opposition, destroy or disgrace it, and thus all of the lesser opposing forces will readily fall. A good example of this is the John Birch Society. The Senate Internal Security Subcommittee released its document, "The New Drive Against the Anti-Communist Programs" in 1961, which spoke directly about the Communists' concern over the awakening anti-Communist forces in this Nation. The Senate Committee report showed how the John Birch Society was singled out by the Communists as an organization to disgrace. The report stated:

Never, since the most virulent days of Goebbels' "hate" propaganda, has anything appeared in the United States comparable to a 47-page booklet, dated June, 1961, put out by the Communist Party of the United States in connection with its drive to smother the expanding anti-Communist movement in this country.

The 35-cent booklet is entitled, "The Fascist Revival," and purports to tell "the inside story of the John Birch Society." The author is Mike Newberry, another Worker-specialist in unbridled smear.

The booklet is evidence of the degree to which the Communist Party considers itself immune from libel, through a complex legal barrier it has built around itself, and by exploitation of the double standard. Communists have created an atmosphere in which those victimized by its lies feel it is futile to seek recompense.

The virulent tone of the booklet, with all stops out in vituperative propaganda, indicates that the Communist Party would like to create a new Pavlovian trigger word for this period in its psychological warfare, and believes "Birchite" might be put into the language this way, replacing "McCarthyite." The impact of the latter fabricated word apparently no longer is strong enough to meet Red needs. Communist deeds have deprived it of its effectiveness in Red "psywar."

The Communists now seek to create a new scare word. This would evoke a conditioned response in a background of fear, founded on the specter of a Fascist plot inside the United States, which would attack all minorities, and spread terror to everyone. This Red propaganda objective is a terror maneuver. It would be what they call the "correct" line for this time, to make the American public jittery through pressure from abroad, by manufactured crises in places such as Berlin and Laos, and by pressure at home through visions of a "Fascist revival." A jittery United States would be off-balance and vulnerable.[9]

Birchite has become a scare word. People who are not aware of the John Birch Society and its functions logically would look upon it as a nutty group if they had no personal contact with the organization. The fact that a legitimate Pro-American organization CAN be downgraded, and such strong negative emotional reactions created within the public, is a clear guide to the effectiveness of programmed negative emotions.

How many of you are aware of the California Senate Fact Finding Report on the John Birch Society? That California committee, headed by Senator Hugh Burns (Dem.), did an extensive investigation of the John Birch Society, and the committee reported to the public:

"We believe that the reason the John Birch Society has attracted so many members is that it simply appeared to them to be the most effective, indeed the only, organization through which they could join in a national movement to learn the truth about the Communist menace and then take some positive concerted action to prevent its spread.

Our investigation and study was requested by the society, which had been publicly charged with being a secret, fascist, subversive, un-American, anti-Semitic organization. We have not found any of these accusations to be supported by the evidence."[10]

How do you like those apples?

Another factor to consider is that certain scare words have lost their effectiveness. "Communism" and "Socialism" are two excellent examples. A decade ago the word Communism had more negative impact upon the public than it does today. Communism is a scare word today only to Conservatives, and that is because they know communism. It is impossible to study communism without developing a strong dislike for what it represents.

When President John F. Kennedy was assassinated, the entire nation was shocked. During the first few hours rather violent emotions were released. Certain influential people stated that the President must have been killed by the "lunatic right," but even without this added stimulus, fantastic emotional acts were vented upon Conservative organizations. Goldwater Headquarters were ransacked, Birch offices were threatened, and in Phoenix, Arizona, shots were fired at the Birch office. The emotional level was high against Conservatives. When it was reported over television that the assassin had been apprehended and that he was a possible Communist, there was a stunned, confused reaction. THE PUBLIC HAD BEEN CONDITIONED TO REACT AGAINST CONSERVATIVES BUT NOT AGAINST COMMUNISTS. If you want proof, try to find one piece of legislation that was submitted to restrict Communist activities. Show me one Communist-front office that was attacked. Show me one Communist Embassy that was picketed.

Certain words can and do trigger emotions. These emotional reactions can trigger people into acting without thinking. When a person becomes emotionally involved, he may lose his ability to reason.

Conservatives also have words which trigger them. I've seen good friends who, when triggered, react almost on command. One evening while I was lecturing I mentioned a certain "liberal's" name and the audience groaned. I'm certain they didn't all think groaning was the thing to do . . . . they just did it automatically. The name had triggered them.

Beware of words . . . . don't let them trigger you. Understand how words trigger other people, and avoid phrasing your sentences in such a manner that you bring about strong emotional reactions. USE words . . . . don't let them use you.

(See Appendix II for a more detailed analysis of "trigger" effects and "unnatural reactions.")

CHAPTER V

A LIBERAL LOOK AT CONSERVATIVES

Have you ever asked yourself, what is a Conservative? Or better still, why am I a Conservative? Why do I think the way I do, react the way I react, or act the way I act?

All of us who profess to wear the Conservative garb should know some of the answers to these questions. I contend that not enough of us ask ourselves these questions often enough or try to answer them.

I make no claim to being a psychiatrist, psychoanalyst, doctor, witch doctor or crystal-ball-gazer. I leave that to the collectivist mentality. I can, however, through just good old-fashioned horse-sense, much study and exposure to Conservatives over an extended time, (not to mention I'm married to one), make a few observations on what makes us tick. Why is this knowledge important? *It is vital because our mental make-up has a direct bearing upon how we discuss issues with our friends.* Knowledge about ourselves and how we react to given situations and word stimuli can mean the difference between winning converts or chasing people farther into the collectivist camp.

You may be assured that the Communists are well aware of how we act or react under given conditions. They take advantage of our reactions at every opportunity, trying to use our energy to their advantage or channeling our energies into paths which will dissipate our effectiveness.

Well, what is a Conservative?

I contend that most Americans are fundamentally conservative. Most Americans want to conserve morality, conserve their reputations, conserve this Nation and our institutions, conserve their family ties, and conserve our Christian ethics.

In fact, there are many people who call themselves political liberals who are conservative in their private lives.

This chapter is basically written for the informed active anti-Communist Conservative.

I shall attempt to point out certain characteristics that we . . . . as Conservatives, have. These characteristics are basic fibres of our nature and affect our actions and reactions. These fundamental Conservative beliefs are the corner-stones on which we base our actions.

In the previous chapter we talked some about the word "conservative" and how people react towards it. Now let's talk about people who are Conservative.

I'll start out, making matters even more confused, by stating that we have two distinct kinds of Conservatives . . . . the Jeffersonian (Liberal) Conservative, and the Classic Conservative. In many ways we are as alike as two peas in a pod, but in others we differ greatly. Today we both carry the label of Conservatism. The Jeffersonian Conservative may have classic Conservative overtones, and vice versa, but before this dissection becomes chaotic, let's discuss the differences.

First, the Classic Conservative: This person is what the name implies . . . . a Conservative. He is slow to act. He mulls ideas over and over, exploring all ramifications before he acts. A Classic Conservative is not gregarious. He usually has a few solid friends whom he treasures. He dislikes large gatherings, and when given a chance will avoid them. He hates giving speeches or projecting his ideas to others. He likes to be left alone and likes leaving others alone. Once he has found something that works for him, he adheres to it tenaciously. A Classic Conservative has a strong ethical base . . . . things are right or wrong, true or false, good or bad. In other words to him there is not much gray but a lot of black and white. He looks upon himself as a realist. You couldn't call a Classic Conservative an out-and-out optimist by any means, but it would be unfair to call him pessimistic. He could be either, depending upon the circumstances. He is suspicious of public relations, people, actors, politicians, and extroverts in general. He is solid, bed-rock and dependable.

A Jeffersonian (Liberal) Conservative is a horse of another color. He generally is an optimist. He has the ability to see the light side of everything. He usually will have a good sense of humor. He is an idealist. His goals are always high and sometimes not too practical. He likes people, likes crowds, is gregarious and outward-going. He would rather not, but usually will, give a speech, talk to strangers, accept leadership and instigate programs.

He is willing to take a chance, because he believes optimism and work can carry it off. He likes new things. He thinks contemporarily on material matters. He likes public relations and thinks Classic Conservatives are sometimes old-fashioned in how they approach the public.

He is as sound as the Classic Conservative in his principles and also has a deep sense of right and wrong. Quite often Jeffersonian Conservatives and Classic Conservatives clash with each other on how certain programs will best be implemented. They sometimes get mad at each other and can't understand "why" another Conservative would act a certain way.

It is important to recognize that there are different kinds of "Conservatives." It's important in our fight with the collectivist mentality.

Let's now look into areas where Jeffersonian Conservatives or Classic Conservatives are "like" two peas in a pod.

Point I: We Conservatives usually are deeply religious. We believe in an all-powerful God, and we feel a direct responsibility toward Him. We believe that He has plainly established how we should behave upon this earth, and has given us rules, laws, and a code to live by. He has established our relationship with our fellow-man and how we, as His creation, are expected to perform. God tells us in no uncertain terms to love Him and obey Him, or else . . . .

God has given us standards, and as believers we use these standards to evaluate ourselves, our neighbors, our Nation and the world. We believe that evil is a separate and dominant force upon this earth, whose sole function is to separate man from God.

We recognize that only God is all-powerful and all-knowing.

We believe that man is finite and has no right to play God with anybody.

Point II: We are individualists. We respect the integrity of other individuals and expect this in return. We believe man controls his social environment, not the other way around.

Point III: We feel responsible for our own actions. We usually look to ourselves when something goes wrong instead of finding someone or something to blame.

Point IV: We are self-supporting. Generally we

take care of ourselves and our own, and expect others to do the same. We like to help others when they ask for help, but would consider it both rude and debasing to interject ourselves into their lives without their express desire. We vigorously resent others who attempt to play God and Godfather to those who don't want it.

Point V: We respect authority. We are taught from childhood to respect our parents, our teachers, our American institutions, our Constitution, our Church. We are impressed by those who through study and self-sacrifice, gain positions of authority. We believe these positions of authority should be used honorably and with dignity.

Point VI: We come to conclusions. Because of our moral standards, we evaluate what we hear, read, and study. Based upon what knowledge we have, we sift, assess and come to conclusions. People who come to conclusions rarely ask questions . . . . they make statements, emphatic statements. I might add, this "coming to conclusions and making statements" aspect of the Conservative is of key significance. It affects his whole attitude in conversations.

Point VII: We try to be truthful. Usually we try to answer every question posed to us. When asked, we feel a compulsion to state our views. We are sometimes aware that what we believe may not be "popular," but we feel that if we don't answer, we are not being moral. Often we carry this too far.

We dislike those who lie and look upon prevaricators as people of weak character. We are not compatible with "professional politicians" who twist the truth glibly and bend it to fit a certain audience. They make us very apprehensive.

Point VIII: We tend to be emphatic individuals. Right's right and wrong's wrong. Black's black and white's white. We generally speak our piece in a few words (most often in the form of a statement). Diplomacy is not an art to which we pay much attention.

Point IX: We are impatient. A well-informed

Conservative finds himself doing a lot of things he would rather not do. He participates heavily in politics, attends meetings, gives speeches, and finds himself in a position of having to inform others on the nature of communism. The prime concern of a Conservative is "let's get this country shaped up so I can get back to doing what I did before." He's in a hurry.

The idea that this is a long-range project isn't too appetizing to his conservative palate; in fact, it's downright distasteful. He becomes extremely impatient with others who aren't doing their part. They are a constant source of frustration to him. "What's WRONG with them? Can't they SEE what's going on?" he impatiently inquires.

A Conservative usually under-estimates his own abilities and intelligence. He often asks: "If I am bright enough to see the problem, why can't others?"

Point X: Conservatives anger easily. We might not always visibly show our anger, but you can often count on it being somewhere inside us. Why do we anger? Simple . . . . when you combine our knowledge with our conclusions, add our strong sense of right and wrong, sprinkle in our impatience and put us into a situation where we are conversing with an individual who thinks everything is "peaches and cream," you're going to have an angry Conservative on your hands.

Point XI: We many times give the impression of being dogmatic, self-righteous, overbearing, and often develop the "either you're with me or you're against me" complex. Because of our convictions, we frequently seem overbearing; in other words, we sometimes come on like the wrath of God. Because of our impatience, we often appear dogmatic. We have a strong sense of individual and national morality; it is a vital factor to us. Generally we bring this into our conversations and sometimes, if we don't watch how we project our position, others draw the conclusion that we are "holier than thou."

A LIBERAL LOOK AT CONSERVATIVES

Christ was the only one who could say, "He who is not with me is against me." (Luke 11:23) When we develop this kind of attitude toward our less-informed friends (and we often do), we literally close the door to useful communications. People are "with us" by the intelligent way we inform.

Point XII: We abhor all forms of totalitarianism. We have a deep-seated distrust for those who carry the banner heralding the omnipotence of any form of government. We have faith in the individual because we believe society is formed of individuals. We believe in the uncommon man, and we believe he only becomes "common" when he grants divinity to demagogues.

We are FOR freedom . . . . thus we must oppose any negative program which subverts free men. History has proven conclusively that the dictator can dictate only when he has a centralized government to enforce his demands.

POWER DOES corrupt and absolute power DOES corrupt absolutely.

We become distraught when we see good people gravitating towards the siren call of centralized government. Our minds project to the inevitable conclusion of such folly . . . . and we shudder.

XIII: We deem ourselves fortunate to have been exposed to such great minds as Thomas Jefferson, Ludwig von Mises, and E. Merrill Root. The solid thought that these men project offers the mind solid food in a sea of pablum.

We find it difficult to refute the soundness of a Frederic Bastiat,[11] and we have yet to find the collectivist who has even tried (and remained a collectivist).

We Conservatives believe that in a more complex world the degree of freedom a man possesses is in direct proportion to the responsibility, integrity and accurate knowledge of the individuals composing the society in which he lives.[12]

Ignorance is the pliable putty of the demagogue.

CHAPTER VI

"EGAD......HERE COMES CARRY NATION!"

Deep down in my heart I feel a great deal of compassion for the newly awakened anti-Communist. When a normal, everyday 24-carat American discovers that everything isn't "peaches and cream" and that our country is in deep trouble, he goes through a truly traumatic experience .... to say the least! He is really something to watch. In fact, you can almost predict the stages a person will go through.

The first is "The Awakening." This stage is of short duration. Some good friend or casual acquaintance slips him a piece of "light" reading, such as Robert Morris' NO WONDER WE'RE LOSING,[13] or John

Stormer's NONE DARE CALL IT TREASON.[14] Our good
friend takes the book without much comment or
even too much interest. He probably has received
the book from a hard-core Conservative friend,
whom I like to refer to as "one of the fastest
pamphlets in the West."

Our friend takes the book home, drops it on a
table, and promptly forgets all about it. One evening,
by chance, the local TV programming isn't up to
par, so he picks up the book for a little educational
light reading. Four hours later, his eyes dilating and
his breath coming in short gasps, it dawns upon
him, "Gad, if this is true . . . . we're in deep trouble!"
That night is a restless one. The next day he seeks
out the friend who gave him the book, and asks him
if he has anything that substantiates what he has
just read.

"The fastest pamphlet in the West" always has
a second book on hand, and the "newly awakened"
can't wait until work is over so he can resume his
reading. He polishes off the second book by early
evening. After another sleepless night, deep reflec-
tion, anguished thoughts, and typical American concern for his country, our friend comes to a decision:
"I've got to do something about this!" Our good
friend has discovered that Communists are really
evil personified, that he has been taken in, and that
he better get busy. He is now in the second stage . . . .
"Carry Nation."

The next day, armed with his newly acquired reading material, he descends upon his place of employ-
ment (or his close friends), with all the aplomb of
a Mack truck. He grabs the nearest person, waves
the book under his nose, and declares: "Wake up!
We've got problems with Commies. YOU'VE GOT TO
READ THIS BOOK!" Our "Carry Nation" is peddling
bad news; he's out of character with what his friends
have known him to be . . . . a week ago he was
happy-go-lucky and now he is "The Avenger."

An argument usually starts at this point. "Well,
old pal, asks his friend, "Where are all these Com-

munists you're talking about?" Our newly-informed anti-Communist is now two-book wise, and suddenly finds himself confronted with arguments he has never encountered before. After a brief bit of sputtering, he exclaims: *"Good grief, man, they're* EVERYWHERE."

His friend, who has been pre-conditioned against right-wing extremists ranting about Communists, exclaims pitifully to himself, "Horrors, my pal's over the hill . . . . flipped his trolley . . . . he's an extremist!"

Our newly-informed anti-Communist bashes his head into one stone wall after another, ricocheting from friend to friend. Nobody seems to listen. He is trying the force-feeding method of education, which consists of grabbing his friend by the lapels and stating: "You've got to read this book!"

The tragedy is that our newly-informed anti-Communist is right! We do have a problem. The material that he has been reading is correct and well documented. But "Carry Nation" has run smack into the result of insidious conditioning of the American public to reject anti-Communists as extremists. He is unaware of all of this; that what he analyzes as apathy and lack of concern on the part of his friends is nothing more than the result of this conditioning process.

So our friend goes into a third stage . . . . "Depression." "It's too late . . . . it's all over . . . . NOBODY cares."

At this point, he backs off from trying to awaken people. "What's the use," he says. "They deserve slavery!" Melancholy sets in. Whenever he hears the "Star-Spangled Banner," he gets a far-away look in his eye. He also gets a bit cynical. He says to himself, "You might go down the tubes, but not me." He starts to look around in Army Surplus Stores for camping gear. He asks his wife to look into food that can be stored for a long time. They decide that this year, instead of spending their vacation at the beach: "We'll camp out in the

mountains or the local woods with the kiddies. Let's
get back to nature." Our friend starts doing exer-
cises to get back into condition. He avoids fatty
foods (bad for hiking) . . . . he even considers giving up smoking (bad for the wind).

All this time the new Conservative continues reading. He becomes more and more informed on the
nature and tactics of our country's enemies. He
reads everything he can lay his hands on; he finds
others who feel the same way he does, and slowly,
but surely, he matures into the fourth stage . . . .
"the knowledgeable, articulate pro-American anti-
Communist."

Our new Conservative recognizes by this time how
many pine cone nuts it takes to feed a growing boy.
He recognizes that nothing can be gained by giving
up and heading for the hills. He is cognizant by now
that the Communist-Socialist movement is directed
by a dedicated, conspiratorial few whose sole cover-
ing is deceit, confusion, criminality and lies. He
recognizes that Communism CAN be defeated by a
properly informed citizenry, and so he sets to work.
He is, by this time, aware of the insidious conditioning process that has taken place on his good friends
and neighbors, and so he INTELLIGENTLY starts to inform and, I might add . . . . win!

CHAPTER VII

A CONSERVATIVE LOOK AT LIBERALS

We Conservatives have a tendency to classify as Liberals all those who disagree with us. I believe that this term is too broad to be descriptive. I dislike categorizing people, but unfortunately people have a tendency to categorize themselves. For the sake of clarity, it is necessary to define a few of the slots that Americans fall into.

Let's talk about by far the biggest segment of the American population, the lovable "Fuzzy."

"FUZZIES"

A "Fuzzy" is your friend and mine. He may be a next-door neighbor whom you like, a bridge partner

44

of long standing, a golf buddy, a business acquaintance, a close relative, a nice guy. A Fuzzy is a person who loves to talk to you about everything, including religion, politics, and Communism, and when perchance you do broach these subjects, he will unknowingly parrot the left-wing clichés. He is a person who never has taken the time to notice the contradictions in his own arguments. He has accepted certain dogmas, believing full well that they are his own ideas.

A Fuzzy loves his country and its institutions deeply. The problem is that he doesn't believe, or at least doesn't want to admit, that anyone would want to corrupt these institutions or could possibly succeed in doing so. He takes great comfort in the slogan, "It can't happen here."

A Fuzzy resents your trying to awaken him to the realities of life. He is prone to accept any argument that seems to decimate the Conservative position, including the time-worn left-wing tactic of name-calling.

Our Fuzzy friends like to think of themselves as rational, sensible political moderates. They religiously vote every election for ALL the candidates of their party. They often state that they "vote for the man, not the party," but they rarely do. They base their opinion all too frequently on opinion polls, some left-wing rag, which they believe to be honest, or some out-spoken "friend" who usually knows less than they do.

Our Fuzzy friends distrust all politicians and often refer to politics as "too dirty" to get into, but by some strange reason believe a man is suddenly sanctified once he is elected and, by osmosis, acquires a dedication to "the people."

If the Fuzzy is a business man, he usually is ethical, hard-working, and conscientious. He generally runs his business conservatively, gripes about his taxes, but meekly pays them. He's a good father, good companion, and a raving optimist. He's "disturbed" over the International situation, but believes that "those guys" in Washington (whoever they are) will take care of it.

In fact, Conservatives usually make our Fuzzy friend nervous. He dislikes what you say because it sounds too frightening. If cornered, he will avoid what he calls "political conversation" because, being basically a good person, if he accepts what you say, he will HAVE to do something about it.

If our Fuzzy is a woman, she is often active in some community project; she's a good mother and wife, and doesn't have time for all those "deep" subjects with which you seem to be so intensely preoccupied. "Oh," she probably will say, "Let's talk about something that is more pleasant; I leave THOSE matters up to my husband." Her husband, unfortunately, is generally as fuzzy as she.

Ever so often one of our dear Fuzzy friends stumbles across the cold, hard facts, and realizes maybe his Conservative friend wasn't so kookie after all. At that moment of truth, he begins to study and dig into the responsibilities of American citizenship. Before long, he too, is loudly denouncing Communism, Socialism, and other social diseases which infect our Nation.

We should all have great compassion and understanding for our Fuzzy friends, and do what we can to expose them to the truth. Instead of getting mad at them, we should realize that, "There but for the grace of God go I."

"CHINA EGGS"

My grandmother used to have a number of porcelain china eggs around the farm. They were used to encourage the hens in the coop to lay eggs. Grandma would put several of these eggs in a nest and, before long, some hen would settle herself on the eggs and try to hatch them. I guess these porcelain beauties brought out the mother instinct in the barnyard cluckers, because they would set for days on top of these phony eggs, clucking away, trying to hatch them. All they would accomplish was to warm them up a bit. As soon as the hen would leave the nest, the china eggs would cool off.

I contend that today a sizeable number of Conservatives are wasting their time perching on top of china eggs," trying to hatch them into full-fledged fighting eagles. In other words, we all have a few friends to whom we have been feeding material for years, trying to stimulate them into taking an active interest in what's going on. All that we accomplish is to warm them up while we are "perched" upon them. As soon as we leave them alone, they revert to their clammy, cool, procelain nature.

Some people just don't WANT to wake up to what's happening to America. In fact, some people just don't care.

If we ever get our country moving in the right direction again, our china egg friends will be the first to say, "See, I told you there wasn't anything to worry about;" or, "We could have done it better our way."

I have a china egg friend; in fact, I think old Charlie is a classic example of PORCELAINA AMERICANA. I worked on Charlie for almost a year until I finally recognized the porcelain veneer with which old Charlie was coated. I'll bet I handed him at least thirty pounds of books to read. I'm positive that they are now resting, unread, in some dark attic corner of Charlie's house, far out of Charlie's sight, and especially out of sight of any visitor that Charlie might have. ("Can't be too controversial, you know.")

Charlie frustrated me for almost one full year. I even contemplated a unique plan that I thought might awaken him.

Late one night I mentally envisioned this approach.

I'll scare the be-daylights out of him!

Charlie is a creature of habit. He goes to work every morning at 7:55 a.m. and arrives home punctually at 5:42 p.m. He plays bridge every Thursday night, and waters his lawn every Sunday morning at ten. He wears the same garb every Sunday for his pilgrimage to the dicondra .... thongs, a beat-up sweatshirt, frayed shorts and a baseball cap. Charlie's weight has shifted over the past twenty years, and he sort of looks like a relaxed pear, held up by a pair of toothpicks.

My plan was to have a truck race up to my house (which is directly across the street from Charlie's), at 10:05 a.m. on a chosen Sunday morning. The truck would have the United Nations police force symbol attached to the side. In the truck would be several of my friends dressed in U.N. garb with the blue helmets perched upon their heads. The truck would screech to a halt; the troops would leap from the truck, smash in my door, enter and drag me, screaming, from the house.

Charlie, I knew, would stand there stupefied, taking it all in.

At a strategic moment, I would break away, dash madly across the street screaming loudly, "I TOLD YOU SO, CHARLIE .... SAVE ME !"

I would then throw myself to the ground at Charlie's knees, hold his legs transfixed so he couldn't move, while my U.N. buddies took pot shots at me, the escaping prisoner. I can mentally picture Charlie now, spraying water everywhere as he desparately tries to disengage himself from my vise-like grip upon his boney, shaking knees.

After chuckling to myself, I immediately dismissed the thought. It might have worked, but I doubt it. After Charlie found out it was a hoax, he would then be convinced beyond all reasonable doubt that his neighbor across the street was the nut he thought he was.

At this point, I hope that no one misunderstands me, because I like Charlie; basically he is a fine man. Like many others, there is something in Charlie's character make-up that makes him oblivious to the issues of the day.

The point I want to make is that we have to

evaluate some of our friends. If they are "china eggs," don't waste valuable time on them. There are plenty of people who are ready to take an active part in the anti-Communist fight if they are properly approached.

It is often comfortable to approach "china eggs." They rarely argue with you; they usually nod their heads in agreement. It's touchier to approach people you know casually, or those you don't know at all. Don't waste your precious time on those who really don't care. Besides, if by some strange fate you "hatched" one of your china egg friends, he would probably be chicken anyway.

"THE AMERICAN LIBERAL"

I differentiate a contemporary American Liberal from a Socialist. The latter I don't care much for, the former I generally like. Before my contemporary Conservative friends start a movement to drum me out of the lodge, let me define the differences.

Many fine people in America today consider themselves "Liberals." They work for Liberal candidates. Many are active in some organization in which the Conservatives wouldn't be caught dead. A few are lawyers who belong to the American Civil Liberties Union. Some are businessmen who are local promoters of the United Nations, and some are active spokesmen for a local, state or national issue which promotes the equality of man through government planning.

Most of these Liberals are intelligent people who are college graduates, and solidly manifest a sincere interest in their fellow man. They honestly look upon themselves as contemporary thinkers who are well read, and have a solid understanding of what's happening at home and abroad.

They look upon us (Conservatives) as being old-fashioned, self-centered, and to some degree, reactionary.

Many of these Liberals are very successful businessmen, lawyers, doctors, and professional people.

Much to the chagrin of Conservatives, they are glib of tongue, forceful and articulate, and seem to have the uncanny ability to constantly put most Conservatives in a defensive position in a political discussion.

Deep down inside, they have an aversion to excessive government, but they believe that if it gets too bad, it can be voted out. They believe that we, as Americans, totally control our government, and that government is a vehicle to promote all good things.

They talk about Communism, but as a group are TOTALLY unaware of how it works. They have accepted all of the information from the State Department as gospel and view the New York Times as the mecca of all good news.

They have been so indoctrinated into "Liberalis Mentalis" that to question their present views and admit they could be wrong would severely shake them. They have a vested emotional interest in liberalism. Admitting to themselves that they could be promoting harmful programs would be unthinkable.

They dislike totalitarianism intensely and they believe that our government is incapable of it, and anyone (that's us) who questions "our" government is definitely capable of totalitarianism.

It is a common, and I might add incorrect, assumption on the part of Conservatives that these Liberals don't read and are uninformed. The fact is they do read, but unfortunately what they have read has been in a basically liberal vein. Many Liberals are liberal because they have manifested an interest in world affairs, and at the time the only readily available reading material was liberally oriented. If you don't believe me, just think back to the 1940's. There wasn't any Conservative or factual anti-Communist material available in any quantity.

The sources these people accepted as factual had a great deal to do with pre-conditioning them against Conservative publications and books. When our material did start to permeate the American scene, these people, because of their reading and preconditioning, rejected it sight unseen, or were so inoculated one way that reading our material compared to reading science fiction.

Some Conservatives might disagree with me, but I am firmly convinced that if this country ever gets into a real state of totalitarianism, many of these Liberals will see the light and come out fighting. It might be too late by then, but I'm sure that they will fight anyway.

We, as Conservatives, have a tendency to write these people off and look upon them as "unsavables." I don't agree. They are approachable if we use some understanding and compassion. They have a tendency to write us off as a group of kooks, and avoid us also. I believe the move is ours. We should by now understand why they think the way they do. We have the added advantage of knowing our side as well as theirs. If we Conservatives can keep our tempers and have a little patience, we stand a good chance of putting our points over to the Liberal in such a manner that he will understand.

Some of today's best Conservative anti-Communists were yesterday's Liberals.

I'll say it again. I don't like what they (the Liberals) promote, but I like many of them as individuals.

The dedicated Socialist is a "Liberal" of a different color. He promotes socialist programs, shouting to the sky his love of the underprivileged, while at the same time using these programs to feather his own nest whenever possible. He is a hypocrite of the first order. His general pattern has been that of a first-class failure in everything he has tried, and instead of having the guts to blame himself, he picks on others. This Socialistic song-bird is easy to spot. Basically he dislikes people and the bitterness shows through. He's a phony, a real loser.

The last is the Communist. He uses Liberals, Conservatives, Socialists, Free Enterprise or Gov-

ernment . . . . anything and everything to promote
his control over mankind. He is at best a criminal.
He kills, lies, uses perversion, sex and narcotics,
cheats and promotes hatred at every opportunity,
while he poses as the helper of mankind. He is
clever; he is trained to be that way. To him, the end
justifies the means, and the end is to obtain the
power of life and death over us and our children.

The Communist has contempt for the Socialist. He
feels that if the Socialist isn't smart enough to recognize the fallacies of Socialism, he deserves his
eventual enslavement. In fact, the Communist uses
Socialism as a vehicle to recruit students to Communism. After a period, if the new Communist has
any brains, he recognizes the conspiratorial aspect
of the movement and the utter bankruptcy of Socialism. If the young Communist isn't bright enough
to recognize this, he never advances far in the Communist hierarchy.

I believe that Communists will go down in history
as the vilest group of butchers who ever lived. The
contempt they hold for all American Liberals and
Conservatives alike is astounding. Khrushchev once
stated his feelings for Americans: "We spit in their
faces and they call it dew."

I, for one, recognize spit when I see it . . . .
don't you?

CHAPTER VIII

ANALYZE YOUR AUDIENCE

Charlie Conservative and Johnny Wright were deeply involved in a heated discussion. The subject matter was what some Conservatives refer to as "The Babel on the East River," better known to the general trade as the United Nations.

Putting it mildly, they were dissecting the glass menagerie, pane by pane. Johnny and Charlie were involved in a conservative verbal game called ifs-man-ship, or "*If* you think that's bad, have you heard this?" The object of the game is to assess all the bad news, add up all the *ifs*, and then guess what year the Communists will take over the world.

Johnny and Charlie were having a gay old time.

They were mildly disappointed that their conversation was interrupted. The cab, in which they were riding, pulled to the curb and abruptly stopped.

Johnny and Charlie started to get out of the cab when they noticed that they weren't at their destination.

"Say Cabbie," said Charlie, "This isn't where we were going."

"This is as far as I'm taking you two nuts!" replied the irate driver. "This is my hack and I'd rather be caught dead than haul around a couple of squirrels like you. Wat-d-ya want, *WAR?* Wat's-a-matter wit you guys? Don't you want to *talk* to people? Wat are you . . . . *isolationists* or sumpthin? Ain't two wars enough for you . . . wat-d-ya want, *bombs* going off?"

Johnny and Charlie stood silently on the street corner, speechless. They watched the cab peel away from the curb and disappear around the first corner. The irate cabbie had even refused to accept their money. They were mortified.

Our two Conservative friends had been graphically shown that they had another person in the ifs-man-ship game. The only problem was, the cabbie didn't understand how the game was played.

Both Conservatives were well-informed on the United Nations. They had been exposed to the pros and cons of this august body, and like most people who take the time to do a depth study, they recognized the glaring weaknesses of this organization.

Obviously, they hadn't taken the cabbie into consideration when they were discussing the iniquities of Alger Hiss's brain-child, the U.N.

Probably the only contact the cabbie had ever had with the U.N. was the local media. He hadn't read anything that opposed the U.N. and he obviously had been won over by United Nations propaganda.

Charlie and Johnny were lucky. They found out the hard way the effect their conversation had on the cab driver. They learned a lesson.

What were their mistakes?

First, they weren't aware of the cab driver's presence.

Second, if they were, they assumed he knew as much as they did about the U.N.

Third, they lost an opportunity to inform the cabbie. There were many other things they could have done if they had been aware of their audience, but unfortunately they were not.

What you say does affect others, one way or another, for better or worse. We, as Conservatives, have to develop a better sense of awareness of those around us. We have to understand as much as we can about those we address.

We must decide what we hope to accomplish by our conversations. What are we after? Are we trying to convince the person to whom we are speaking? Are we trying to prove just one specific point? Are we trying to neutralize a liberal argument? Are we trying to sell a listening third party? What's our time element? These are just a few factors that we should take into consideration when we address others. Let's look at some of the other factors to consider in planning a conversation.

The Time Element: Time is an important factor. Look upon your conversation as a person pouring milk into flour. If done properly, the flour will absorb all the milk that you pour. If you do it too fast, much will spill over, and all you will have is a sticky, lumpy mess. If you pour it too slowly, it will dry up and evaporate.

Here is one sticky, lumpy mess that I will always remember. One day I was introduced to a local merchant by a fellow Conservative. I had never met the man before. I could tell that he was emotionally disturbed and pre-occupied by something that had happened before we arrived. He was bursting at the seams to share his feelings with us, so I inquired: "What's wrong? Something seems to be bothering you."

"You bet something's bothering me. My stomach

is a nervous wreck! I have just been subjected to
the worst lunch I've ever had."

"Was the food bad?"

"Food! No . . . . it was the company. Do you know
what they said?" Without waiting for my reply,
he launched into a blow-by-blow account of his
luncheon conversation.

"Why, those nuts I ate with told me that our
State Department was infiltrated with Communists;
our foreign aid worked against our nation's best
interests; we are becoming bankrupt, and there will
soon be a major depression; the Communists are
going to take over our country; and they believe
that our educational system is subverted. They said
that mental health was part of a conspiracy. They
even believed that somewhere in Alaska there's going
to be a concentration camp for anti-Communists. And
to top it all off, they even objected to the water I
drink. Gad, what a couple of nuts. What do you
think?"

"You're right," I replied, "They're nuts!"

This shopkeeper was a good, sound man and obviously not too informed. He had been subjected to
a couple of "Carry Nation" Conservatives, who tried
to give him a two-year educational course in a
twenty-minute lunch. They had not only alienated
this man, but they may have created in him a long-
lasting gastric disorder.

I would like to pose this question to the reader.
Do you think they were effective Conservatives?
How difficult do you believe it will be for anyone to
approach this shopkeeper on any of these subjects
again?

The Time Element . . . . it is very important! It is
a common Conservative mistake to oversell. We
make good points and then proceed to destroy everything we say by over-saturating our audience.
There is a saying among salesmen, "Sampson was
a piker. He killed 1,000 men with the jawbone of an
ass. Every day at least 10,000 sales are killed with
the same weapon."

"Patience" should be one of our best weapons. Wyatt Earp, the famous frontier marshall, was once asked how he survived over one hundred gun fights without a scratch. His reply was, "I drew very slowly . . . . but with haste."

Within that story is an object lesson for Conservatives. Are we trying to neutralize a Liberal? Our chance of converting all Liberals is nil, but if we can prevent them from using left-wing clichés, we have at least stopped them from transmitting harmful propaganda.

If you are capable of shooting down one of their pet clichés, you can be reasonably assured they won't use it again. Nobody (especially a Fuzzy) likes to have his old ego bent out of shape.

How many people do you know who love to argue for the sake of argument? These people generally are wonderful transmission belts for passing on Conservatives' ideas . . . . that is, if they are given a good point or two.

Some people argue PURELY for the sake of argument. They argue liberally to Conservatives and conservatively to Liberals. If you have given them a good Conservative argument, you can bet that they will use it on the first Liberal with whom they come in contact.

Be aware of your audience; understand what you are trying to communicate . . . . then do it. The Conservative who "draws slowly, but with haste" is tremendously effective. In other words ACT, don't REACT; be aware, not unaware.

CHAPTER IX

THE BROAD BRUSH

Be specific. Generalizations have a tendency to work against the persons who use them.

Conservatives get their dander up when a Commentator refers to Conservatives as extremists. Liberals get their dander up when Conservatives refer to Liberals as pinks. Both are justified in their complaints.

Let's skip the "broad brushing" that is used against us, and concentrate on our misuse of generalizations, analyzing the negative effect this has upon our Conservative movement.

As an example, we use the term "government" too loosely. "The government is leading us down the road to Socialism. The government is aiding Communists. The government is becoming totalitarian. The government is rotten to the core, etc., etc."

Most Americans look favorably upon the government because they believe the government is the American people. We are raised to respect our form of government, the Constitution and the Bill of Rights. Americans consider the government to be an extension of the public will, and this is as it should be. Americans take our government for granted, and have forgotten that government, if not constantly restrained, can become the oppressor instead of the servant. So when we, as Conservatives, knock the government, those who don't understand what we mean sometimes feel that we are knocking them personally.

We Conservatives want to conserve our *form* of government, and because we have taken the time to understand how it should work, and how it was intended to work, we naturally are appalled at how it is being perverted.

It is not being perverted by the majority of people in government . . . . just a dedicated few. Most of our government employees are faithful Americans, and when we use the "broad brush" we paint in many people who don't deserve it.

Be specific. Say "There are those in OUR government who are trying to destroy it. A dedicated minority of Socialists and Communists have forced OUR government into the position that . . . ." "Some are manipulating our government, trying to change it so that it will . . . ."

When you say the government is aiding Communists and the person to whom you are speaking voted for the present administration, you are in effect calling him pro-Communist, insulting his patriotism, his good judgment, and putting him in the position of being anti-American.

He probably dislikes aid to Communists as much as you do, but feels a loyalty to our government and believes it knows "what it's doing."

You can be reasonably assured that he doesn't understand subversive tactics, and how a few well-placed conspirators can affect our national policy. By being specific, you can inform him of these subversive tactics, Communist methodology, Socialist planning, etc. Point out to him how Harry Dexter White, as Undersecretary of the Treasury, was extremely instrumental in formulating many policies which hurt our government. Show him the key position held by this identified Communist before he was exposed. Do the same with Alger Hiss. Ask him how effective HE thinks these men were in advancing communist doctrine in this country.

After a while, he will put two and two together without *your doing the addition for him.*

The broad brush alienates . . . . being specific educates.

The general American population has been conditioned to believe that we, as Conservatives, are "against" everything. When we use the broad brush, we fit the picture the left-wing paints of us.

This broad brush also may be used indiscriminately against other American institutions, such as, "The Press doesn't give us the truth!" Or, "Educators are subverting our children." "The colleges are left-leaning." "The Churches promote Socialism." etc. These are Conservative broad generalities which "trigger" people to react against us.

There are those of the Press who manipulate news and don't tell all the truth. *Some* Educators subvert; specific colleges *are* left-leaning; and some Church leaders do promote Socialism . . . . but not *all.* Again, be specific.

We are against any program that subverts our American institutions because we are *for* freedom. Jefferson once stated, "Any fight against tyranny is a positive action."

When we Conservatives resort to "broad brushing," we hurt conservatism, and thus our Nation. BE FACTUAL, BE SPECIFIC.

CHAPTER X

LIKE PEOPLE

Several years ago I attended a local political fund raising feed. All of the party faithfuls were on hand to support this noble cause, and raise a few dollars for the local partisan hero. Many fine women work their fingers to the bone preparing these soirees, hoping to secure a few dollars for their favorite candidate. The candidate usually gets the money and the attention while the unsung heroines of the kitchen get the left over salad.

The gastric attacks that are suffered for the cause of Conservatism magnify during an election year. There are invitations to dinners, luaus, brunches, lunches, teas, cocktail parties, coffee hours, snacks and every imaginable kind of assault upon the digestive system. If, perchance, the hostess does prepare some epicurean delight, the desert is usually a speech that *always* accompanies this kind of gathering.

One of these days some smart politician will send out a letter stating that he is inviting you to a fund-raising feed-fest, but instead of insisting that you attend, he will offer you an alternate plan. He will send out a letter which simply states that after paying the caterer, renting the dining hall, paying for speakers, all he will make on a ten dollar dinner ticket is about two dollars and fifty cents per head, so why not send a check for five dollars for you and your wife, and you and he will both be money ahead. It might work.

This particular fund-raising function sticks in mind because of one small but significant incident. A few college kids were present. They were friends of the host's daughter. They were not conservatively oriented by any means. During the speeches, I kept glancing their way and watching their reactions to what was being said. I could tell that they were rejecting every word. In fact, they thought our speaker was quite laughable. As soon as the talk was over, I made a beeline to them. I wanted to find out why they reacted the way they did. It didn't take me too long to find the ringleader of the group. After I introduced myself and asked a question or two, the young man who was sporting a sparse beatnik-type beard launched into a typical left-wing diatribe against Conservatives.

After nearly one hour of patient discussion, I began to penetrate his left-wing cliches and start him thinking. The diatribe stopped, and he and his friends proceeded to ask legitimate questions. It was an hour well spent. They were good kids who, unfortunately, had never been properly exposed to Conservative philosophy, and they were sincerely interested and intrigued. I spotted in the audience a well-known Conservative whom they all knew by reputation. He is a gentle, considerate person, and I knew that the young bearded Fuzzy would be impressed by him, so I steered the young Liberal through the crowd and introduced him at the first opportunity. The bushy-chinned youth brashly threw a very pointed question at the well-known Conservative. He smiled, but before he could reply, a person sitting at the same table belched out venomously, "You damned beatniks are selling our country out . . . . you've got a nerve asking a question like that, pinko!"

I wanted to strangle "the Conservative" right on the spot. The kid turned on his heel and marched through the crowd, visibly hurt, muttering, "Why did he have to attack me? All I asked was a question. I'll tell you what's wrong with Conservatives . . . . they're name-callers, narrow-minded, etc., etc."

One complete hour shot. In fact, instead of any net gain, this youth was driven deeper into the liberal camp by an unthinking reaction from a "Conservative" who should have known better.

As Christians, we should all know better. It is easy to get mad . . . . but anger is an emotion which gains nothing, especially when it is directed at the individual to whom you are speaking.

We are taught from childhood to respect another man's position, and him as an individual. I can't think of one person I know (except Communists), who have arrived knowingly at their conclusions by dishonorable means, can you?

You may dislike ideas intensely. You may dislike Socialism with a feeling bordering on passion. But if you translate that feeling into a personal dislike for the individual who supports socialist concepts, you have completely shut off any lines of communication. Antagonism toward the individual will show through. Hating individuals is a weapon of our enemies. It is an all-consuming belief in them. Lenin taught hate. He preached it and believed it should be used as a vehicle to bring about world Communism.

Understanding, compassion, empathy, concern for the well-being of others are foundations of our heritage. They are some of our most important tools.

Resentment of an individual will cause a definite negative reaction to your Conservative position. Result . . . . net loss.

If you are a Conservative and blow off and get mad at the slightest provocation, then you have two choices: One is to control your temper and develop tolerance of people and their ideas or, two, do the Conservative cause a big favor by keeping your mouth shut.

CHAPTER XI

ASK QUESTIONS

A man from Massachusetts was once asked: "Why do you people from Massachusetts always answer a question with a question?"

The man from Massachusetts replied: "What do you mean we always answer a question with a question?"

You would think that all Liberals came from Massachusetts after analyzing that joke. How many times have you been in a discussion with a Fuzzy Liberal on some important subject, and before you could bat your eye, found yourself on another subject, then another, and another, ad infinitum? Pretty soon you get the definite impression that he thinks you are against apple pie, baseball and Mom.

What has happened is that your friend hasn't responded at all to your original point or STATE-MENT. He has, in turn, fired a question at you, and while you are trying to answer the first question, has already re-loaded his vocal cannons to fire another.

It doesn't take long before your dander starts to rise, the hair on the back of your neck bristles, and your blood pressure soars.

You have fallen, as usual, into a typical semantic trap where you find you're in a defensive position and losing the discussion.

Let's take a typical situation and analyze it. You're at work and you, the Conservative, make the statement: "Say Charlie, the dirty Commies are really taking over in the world at a rapid rate. We've got to do something about it."

Charlie responds: "What do you mean the Commies? . . . . We've got to clean up the home-front first. Do you go along with the way our old folks are suffering from lack of proper medical attention?" (Change subject, change emphasis, end in question).

"Why are you right-wingers opposed to medicare and helping our sick citizens?"

"MEDICARE! It's Socialism pure and simple" (Statement again) says the Conservative.

Your friend then replies: "What do you have against our government? . . . . They're promoting it. What's the matter, are you against our government? What makes you think you're so smart?" (Questions) And on and on and on . . . .

The Conservative, because of his nature and education, has read about the problems in the world and is angered about the advance of Communism in all countries, but within fifteen seconds after he broaches the subject he finds himself against everything and portrayed as an oppressor of the elderly.

The Conservative unknowingly has just been subjected to left-wing techniques by a friend who

PROBABLY DOESN'T EVEN KNOW HE IS USING THEM.

Many Americans have been programmed slowly and systematically to fire questions at the Conservatives. These questions are geared to put him in a defensive position, and unfortunately the Conservative unknowingly allows it to happen.

Why does he allow this to happen? Why is he constantly back-tracking instead of going on the offense?

There are many reasons. Let's name a few.

First, the Conservative has a strong moral foundation. He has a code of ethics by which he evaluates all he hears and reads. Based upon this, he naturally comes to conclusions. These conclusions invariably are expressed as statements, not questions.

Second, the Conservative's strong stands are generally predictable. He usually argues in a predetermined manner, based upon his prior conditioning . . . . and thus he is easily side-tracked.

Third, when a person is making statements, he has to slow his mind down to the speed of the spoken word, and hence he is easily manipulated by the person who is asking the questions. A person listening can think at least three times as fast as the one who is talking. In other words, a person's mind is often three times faster than his mouth.

Fourth, the Conservative has argued defensively for so long, it has become an ingrained habit pattern. It is a bad habit which we must break.

Fifth, the Liberal has had the habit of asking questions inculcated in him, and hence is always on the offensive (anti-Conservative) . . . . the Conservative is not. (If you don't believe me, strike up ANY conversation on any political subject and watch the cliché questions come flowing out of your Liberal friend's mouth).

There are other reasons and we will cover them in other chapters, but let's concentrate on how we can go on the offensive.

First: Develop the habit . . . . I REPEAT, DEVELOP THE HABIT . . . . of asking questions instead of making statements. If you make a statement, learn how to tack on a question. Questioning a person CAN accomplish many things:

1. You can ascertain the degree of knowledge the person has at his command on any given subject. How are you, as a Conservative, going to educate unless you establish where the educational process has to start? How many times have you talked to people about "foreign aid to Socialist nations" and found out later that the person didn't even know what Socialism is? You have to ascertain the degree of knowledge your friend has, and the only way is to draw him out by asking questions.

2. You control the subject matter and thus the conversation. (more on this in the next chapter)

3. The person being questioned has to think! Only through posing a series of questions can you break through the comfortable wall of clichés so many of our friends have erected around their brains; clichés that have been conveniently supplied to them by the collectivist planners. You have to break through surface knowledge.

Let me give you an example of how it works. Three people were having lunch . . . . one Liberal, two Conservatives. The Conservatives were talking about Communism. Before long the Liberal couldn't take it any more and came pouring into the conversation with both left feet.

"You're all wrong," he emphatically stated, "I know all about Communism. I read *Time, Life, Look,* and keep up on all of this. Where do you get your conclusions? They're contrary to what I read. Are these publications all wrong?"

At this point the Conservatives could have answered typically with "Those publications! Do you believe THOSE Liberal rags? Why do you know that

. . . . etc., etc., etc." Fortunately they didn't. The Conservatives before long would have been put into the position of being "against." To the Liberal they would have been attacking one of America's most cherished institutions, the Free Press. They would have reacted typically, and from that point on nothing positive would have been accomplished. Instead, one of the Conservatives turned to the Liberal and said, "Gee, I'm glad that you know all about Communism. I've had trouble understanding the dialectic mind of the Communist. Would you explain it to me?"

"Huh?" stammered the Liberal.

"Well then," inquired the Conservative, "what do you think is the most dangerous Communist transmission belt in our State?"

"Communist transmission belt? Do they make automotive parts too?" asked the surprised Liberal.

"No, a transmission belt is a front which is used to pass on Communist propaganda to the uninformed public," stated the Conservative. "Which front do you think is doing the most damage in our State?"

By this time the Liberal was totally confused. "I guess I don't know as much about Communism as I thought I did," he honestly admitted. "How do these transmission belts work?" he asked. He was listening to the Conservatives now . . . not reacting.

The Conservatives posed questions. They didn't react. They controlled the conversation, pointed out to their friend his lack of knowledge on the subject of Communism, and intelligently won his attention.

The day Conservatives develop the ability to ask questions and go on the offensive will be the day we really start rolling back Socialism and Communism.

All it takes is practice and patience. Are you willing?

CHAPTER XII

CONSERVATIVE ASTRONAUTS

Several years ago, we launched men into space. The satellites raced around the world at an awesome speed, circling the globe within hours. People were impressed by these fine astronauts who literally established new horizons in man's limited knowledge of space travel.

In the exploration of the outer limits, we Conservatives have overlooked the speed of travel of the "inner limits."

Let me give you an example: You and a Fuzzy friend are discussing the weather, children, and other friendly-type subjects. Everything is peaceful and harmonious. Suddenly that uncontrollable urge comes over you to get into a different area of conversation . . . . International Communism. So, in typical Conservative fashion, you say: "Did you read in the paper today what the Commies are doing in the Congo? I think it's a horrible situation!" (typical Conservative statement)

Your friend responds, "I don't think that's any of our business. . . . They have a right to self-determination. We have problems enough with the poor Negro here at home. Do you approve of the outright bigotry that's going on in Mississippi?" (typical Liberal cliché with question)

You respond with, "Oh, I don't think it's that bad in Mississippi. The people have a right under the Constitution to establish what is best for their State." (Conservative statement)

Your now-ignited friend replies, "Do you mean you go along with the oppression that those Southerners have imposed upon free Negro Americans?" (a heated question)

Etc., etc., etc., etc., and so forth.

You, my friend, have just become an official Conservative Astronaut! You have been taken from the Congo to Mississippi in less than six seconds. Pretty fast travel, if you ask me!

The important subject and the one you wanted to talk about was the Congo situation. *What in the world are you doing in Mississippi?*

Your friend unconsciously changed the subject. His knowledge on the Congo was obviously inadequate or he would have continued with that subject matter. The fault at this point lies at your doorstep, BECAUSE YOU LET HIM CHANGE THE SUBJECT.

Conservatives are constantly falling into this verbal orbit. KEEP YOUR FRIENDS ON THE SUBJECT!

If you allow them to take you from one subject to another, you will never get any of your points across because *you* are allowing them to use every cliché they have at their command. Inevitably, they will throw a barrage of questions at you until they get you into an area where you are not equipped to argue, then pounce upon you and, before you know it, you've been nailed to the wall. You will walk away with the distinct feeling that your friend thinks you are "Count Dracula" while he is the "Standard-bearer of Mankind."

I repeat, keep your Fuzzy Friend on the subject! This sometimes requires patience while they run through their verbal labyrinth. Sometimes it takes a polite interruption, but no matter how you do it, always come back to the original subject until you have completely exhausted your friend's knowledge on that particular matter. This can be done by ending everything you say with a relevant question.

When you keep your friend on the subject matter, he has to think beyond his surface knowledge to compete in the conversation. When this happens, he isn't reacting as he has been conditioned to react .... and that is what you are after.

It is only when your friend mentally admits that he doesn't know much about that particular subject that he will possibly listen or admit that you have pertinent information that is important to him.

Most people don't like to arrive at new conclusions. Subconsciously, the old ego factor takes over, and if you keep them on the subject matter *too* long, you will ruffle their tail feathers. When you see this happening, back off a bit, compliment your friend's intelligence, and offer him a book to read on the subject you've been discussing. Say something like, "Charlie, I know you are vitally interested in this subject. I have a book that would help fortify your knowledge on this matter and, besides that, I sure would appreciate your comments on this 'document'."

If you want to see a book snapped up in a hurry, try that approach. One thing you do want is your friend's opinion. If you have just pinned him on this particular subject, you can bet your bottom depreciated dollar he doesn't want to be boxed again.

If you can get your friend to read, a big chunk of the battle is won.

Another point: Conservatives often bite on the tempting bait offered by a new channel of conversation. You probably know something about that subject too, so you easily follow along. That's another trap. At best, all you will be doing is matching tit-for-tat . . . . liberal cliché, conservative cliché, liberal cliché, conservative cliché.

Conservatives also have the darndest compulsion to answer every question that's asked of them, and while they are trying to think up answers, the Fuzzy is thinking up a new cliché to shove down their throat. A person can talk at a certain speed, but again, the mind works at about three times that speed. So, while you're talking (making statements), they're thinking up another cliché.

Next time, take a good look at the person with whom you are conversing. Nine times out of ten, he isn't really listening. He's waiting for you to shut up so he can pose another cliché question.

The moral of this chapter is: "Don't be a Conservative Astronaut and take those fanciful flights from one liberal cliché to another. Find your subject and stick to it!"

CHAPTER XIII

NAME DROPPING
(Use Authorities)

Quite a few years ago, I was invited to give a lecture on "Communist Front Tactics" to a group of interested citizens in an adjoining city. One of the hostesses decided to invite a rather large group of people over to her house for a social hour before the lecture to meet my wife and me.

After a few formal introductions, I gravitated to the snack bar and located myself strategically near the creamed cheese dips. I struck up a conversation with another cheese-dip fancier and, while we merrily dunked potato chips into the rapidly disappearing delicacy, we argued on everything from soup

74

to nuts. The only thing we agreed upon was the quality of the cheese dip.

Before long, we had to leave for the lecture hall. My cheese-dip friend and I had a gay old time discussing the issues of the day. As I walked out of the door, I could hear his wife saying to him, "Dear, did you have a good time talking to the speaker for tonight?" *"Speaker!"* was his shocked reply. "Do you mean I was arguing with the *speaker?"*

When I arrived at the hall, he was waiting for me, and I had no sooner got my foot out of the car than he started apologizing profusely. I was embarrassed. I just couldn't get it across to him that I had enjoyed arguing with him, and what difference did it make, anyway, if I was the speaker?

Later on it dawned on me. What I had said at the party as far as he was concerned was just one man's opinion, but when he found out that I was an AUTHORITY on the subject, it made all the difference in the world.

The funny part about this whole thing is that this lecture was the first one I had ever given on that particular phase of Communism. I was roped into giving the talk because of the persuasiveness of a good friend. They needed a speaker that night, and I was the pigeon. The club, with the help of good publicity, built me up as an expert so that they could turn out a good audience. I know ONE person who believed the advance propaganda.

The point is, from our earliest days we, as Americans, are taught to respect legitimate authorities .... our Teachers, our Ministers, our Officials. It is an integral part of our American fibre. The Liberals know this. They are constantly creating "Authorities" out of thin air on this and that, so they can feed their propaganda to us through "reputable" sources. The Communists set up "fronts" for this purpose, and always get a Professor, Minister, or "highly-rated" individuals to add authenticity and respect to their programs. The general public isn't aware of this devious tactic, and unquestioningly accepts these so-called authorities.

The Conservative rarely takes advantage of Americans' respect for authority. We must develop the ability to quote reliable authorities. A Conservative will read a book such as Robert Morris' "No Wonder We Are Losing,"[13] and then proceed to expand on the facts given to him in this book on his own knowledge. He will come to conclusions and it will usually appear in conversation in this manner:

"Sam, do you know that Communists have been working in this country for a long time? Why, they were even in New York in 1940 in the Teachers' unions!" (Conservative statement)

The person to whom our Conservative friend is trying to communicate could reasonably conclude, "Well, that's your opinion . . . . so what?"

If this same statement could have been worded possibly in this manner, "You know, Sam, the other day I finished reading 'No Wonder We Are Losing,' written by Judge Morris who, as you probably know, was former Chief Council for the Senate Internal Security Subcommittee. He is recognized as one of the Nation's top authorities on Communist subversion, and he stated that in the State of New York, in 1940, that . . . ."

Sam, at this time, has a hard time saying, "So what?" It has been presented as an authority's opinion . . . . not yours. Sam is now in the position of arguing against Judge Robert Morris . . . not you.

This is what I mean by name-dropping. Learn to use legitimate authorities in your conversations. The hardest people to convince are all too often your closest friends and acquaintances. It is difficult for them to believe that you might know more about anything (especially politics or Communism) than they do, so when you try to convince them YOU know more, you are literally trying to be a prophet in your own country.

A person could actually bring someone who knew

less about the subject than you do, introduce him as an authority on the issue in question, and your "authority" would be believed before you would. This is just human nature, the old ego at work again, that brings on this phenomenon.

Your chance of convincing somebody who doesn't know you too well is actually better than trying to convince a relative. Since a stranger doesn't know you, he is far more willing to accept you as an authority on a subject if you approach it properly and sound knowledgeable. Now is the proper time for "name-dropping."

"The other day I attended a lecture by so-and-so and he stated . . . ."

"The last House Committee report on Communist tactics states . . . ."

"J. Edgar Hoover, in his report to the Congressional Committee on Labor, said . . . ."

"Herb Philbrick, who served nine years in the Communist Party for the FBI, stated that . . . ." etc.

This establishes that you study and have reliable source material. In essence, it sets you up as a serious student of Communism, and possibly as an authority. We have many outstanding authorities to quote . . . . let's use them.

As a word of warning, don't give the impression of, "I'm smart and you're stupid." No one appreciates a know-it-all. . . . That's the first lesson in "How to lose friends." Don't ever fib . . . . know your sources. Truth is a great weapon and doesn't have to be "improved" upon; all you have to do is present it properly.

Next time you find yourself in a discussion with friends about Communism, drop names of authorities freely. When you combine this with, "What do you think?" (a question), and then keep your friends on the subject, you will be much more effective than when just expressing your opinion.

CHAPTER XIV

HUMOR

Humor, I sometimes believe, is becoming a lost art. A good old-fashioned belly laugh relaxes the bones and lets the sunshine through. It also helps you keep your perspective.

Poking fun at a particular set of dogmatic beliefs is an age-old American custom. Modern Liberals, in their attempts to be serious, are sometimes down-right hilarious and, at times, so are Conservatives.

One of the tragedies of today is that certain jokes are no longer considered in "good taste." Dialect jokes are an example. If you tell a joke in an Irish, Negro, Jewish, English, Scotch, Chinese, Japanese,

Southern, or Brooklyn dialect, you can be categorized as "anti" that specific group. You almost get the feeling that you will be "investigated" by some pressure group if you do tell a dialect joke. A joke is in bad taste only if it actually debases some segment of our society. The mere use of a particular dialect is not debasement.

Conservatives sometimes become so wrapped up in the seriousness of the problems facing our Nation that they lose sight of the power of humor, not to mention its medicinal effects.

A good Conservative friend of mine came charging up to me one day waving a newspaper article .... he had mayhem in his eye.

"Bill, did you read this? Get a load of this propaganda! Have you ever seen such outright lies? Read it .... go ahead .... just read it!"

He thrust the article under my nose, muttering, "GO AHEAD, just read that!"

By this time I had the distinct feeling he wanted me to read the article, so taking the paper from his shaking hand I started to read.

It was written by one of the local starry-eyed socialists of sophomoric sentimentality. The writer in question was typical of the self-anointed saviours of humanity. In about fifty per cent of his articles he carries the torch for the brotherhood of man and the fatherhood of government. In the other fifty per cent of his articles, he condemns those whom he considers anti-brotherhood of man. In other words, anyone who dares to take a position to the right of Adlai Stevenson.

The article dealt with the "paranoia" of the radical right (unnamed but implied), the manic-depressive tendencies of said groups, and the inability of these people to grasp the complexities of this enlightened world. The article was frothy to the point of being a bit hysterical. The author ended his vitriolic assault upon the Conservative community by stating that calmness, love and reason should prevail. This struck me as being hilariously funny, and so I did what came naturally . . . . laughed. My Conservative friend didn't get the point. "What's so blankety-blank funny?" he asked.

I pointed out the glaring contradiction in the article and why I considered it so humorous. After a moment of consideration, my friend stated, "You know, that article is a bit ridiculous." Then he chuckled a bit also.

A few days later I again met my buddy. He had a big smile all over his Conservative countenance and was in a visibly rare mood. The contrast from our last encounter was startling.

"Why the big grin, Sam?" I asked.

"Well, Bill, you know that article I showed you? I had shown it to several people before I saw you, and wound up in a few hot debates. I guess I was mad because I hadn't gotten anywhere with these people. After I left you, I showed the article to some more people and pointed out its incongruous aspects, and I'll be darned if they all didn't see the ridiculous nature and the humorous contradictions in the article. You know, Bill, maybe we should all laugh a bit more at these comics."

I agree. I don't think we should slap our sides in merriment every time a left-wing pundit opens his mouth; but we should recognize that humor is a powerful tool and the left-wingers are constantly dropping big FAUX PAS into our laps, which we can use to point out the ridiculousness of their position. The left-wing establishment constantly pokes fun at the Conservative . . . . we should poke a bit in return. If you want to see an ultra-southpaw ignite like a roman candle, poke a little fun at his pet dogmas.

"ANALOGIES"

Through humor you have a wonderful vehicle to inform your friends. Unfortunately, people remember humorous situations a lot longer than they remember cold, hard facts.

As an example, one friend of mine when discussing the United Nations uses a very effective and humorous analogy. He asks:

"What would you think if J. Edgar Hoover sat down with the Mafia to discuss crime and law enforcement. Then, after they all got together, the good guys and the bad guys, J. Edgar stated, 'Some of your people are up in the hills making booze . . . . let's go up there and get them!' And then the Mafia looked up, smiled, and vetoed."

Simply stated . . . . That's the U.N. People will remember that simple analogy.

Tom Anderson, President of Southern Farm Publications, is a masterful story-teller who ties humorous situations to present-day conditions. Because of this ability, he is in constant demand as a writer and lecturer. Some of the analogies Mr. Anderson uses are classics and should be told time and time again.

The next time you hear a good joke, anecdote or analogy, remember it and use it. You will be surprised how some jokes that at first don't seem to relate to the Conservative humorous weapon system can be modified to work.

A friend of mine reminded me of a wonderful old analogy that Abraham Lincoln used to prove a point. The point he was trying to prove doesn't apply today, but the analogy is extremely contemporary if properly used.

Mr. Lincoln asked his friend, "If you call the tail of a dog a leg, how many legs would a dog have?" His friend answered, "Five, of course!" "No," said Lincoln, "you can call the tail of a dog a leg, but that doesn't make it one."

My friend uses the same analogy, but instead of a dog, uses an elephant. Then he relates the joke to certain ultra-liberal so-called "Republicans" and asks, "Isn't it true you can call so-and-so a Republican, but does that make him one?" (Harry Bridges has registered as a Republican, but I doubt if it made him one philosophically).

There is an old expression, "Nobody likes a sour mouth." Did you ever ask yourself, "Do I come on like the wrath of an enraged bull when I approach my friends? Does my concern for my country so encompass me that I lose my perspective and become *overly*-emotional when I talk about Communism and Socialism? Have I lost my ability to laugh at situations and myself?"

If that's the case, instead of helping the Conservative movement, you probably hinder it.

Never in our Country's history has so much depended upon rational thought. Emotional love of country is a wonderful thing, but if we are incapable of controlling our emotions and they control us, our job of communicating is all the more difficult.

Ask yourself, *have I ever won anybody to my point of view when I was mad?*

A sense of humor definitely relaxes. A joke in good taste keeps a friendly conversation going. Our job is to convince people there is a serious problem and jar them into taking an active role in solving it. Humor can help if you use it properly . . . . and it will help you feel better at the same time. Remember, sour-mouths never win.

CHAPTER XV

DOUBLE STANDARDS AND FALSE PREMISES

The Conservative misses a good bet when he doesn't develop one good mental habit. It is the habit of looking for the double standard in the left-wing argument. By double standards I don't mean that their standards are twice as good as ours. I mean that their positions are almost always contradictory.

Before you read another line, put down this book and try to think up as many left-wing double standards as you can remember.

Welcome back. I hope you had fun. If you couldn't think of many, then you haven't been using your brain cells, or worse, you haven't been reading.

Most liberal arguments are as "holey" as swiss cheese. When you point out the double standards to your friends and then drive the point home, it can be one of your best methods of awakening them.

I'll list and discuss some basic liberal double standards for you to cogitate and expand upon, and then its up to you to apply them in discussions.

Little dictators—big dictators. It's perfectly all right to denounce little dictators like Franco, Salazar and Batista, but we have to negotiate, co-exist and get along with big dictators (Tito, Mao Tse-Tung, Khrushchev and successors).

To investigate—not to investigate. It's pro-American to investigate labor racketeers, big business, and "monopolies," but it's un-American and witch-hunting to investigate Communists, Communist frontiers, and corruption in government.

United Nations or Bust. It is the "enlightened" thing to do to denounce Tshombe and send troops to Katanga, but it was not the "enlightened" thing to send troops to Hungary in 1956. The U.N. is supposed to fight world criminality, but it gives membership and veto power to the world's biggest criminal.

Social programs. The planners believe that government should take care of people. When asked why, they say people won't take care of themselves. The question I now ask is, "If these people won't take care of themselves, then how can we expect them to use good judgment in the election of individuals to run this 'moral Government'?"

How do you get moral programs out of immoral people? If they say that most people are moral, then I ask, "Why do we then need these social programs, because if the public is moral, then they will meet their responsibilities as individuals. Then who needs social programs?"

Economic double-talk. If an individual American spends more money than he takes in, he winds up bankrupt. Since government is no more than an extension of individual Americans, how can our

Government create prosperity by spending more than its income?

I could go on and on. There are many, many more examples of double standards. I hope you will start looking for them in your conversations with others and begin pointing them out to your friends. Develop a mental habit of looking for the double standard. It is usually there.

"THE FALSE PREMISE"

Beware of the false premise. If you get caught on the horns of a false premise, you can forget your chances of convincing anyone.

A false premise is an inaccurate or falacious foundation. When a Conservative unknowingly accepts a false premise as a truism then he, in effect, has built his own cross. You don't have to worry about nailing yourself to it because your liberal friends will do it quite effectively.

Accepting a bad premise is a common Conservative error. It is utterly impossible to educate when you work from a bad premise.

Communists and Liberals almost always use flawless logic, but the conclusions are false because the logic is based on a plausible but false premise.

How in the world can you discuss Communism intelligently if you accept the premise that communism is nationalistic and not international? How can you discuss the evils of socialism if you accept the premise that a little bit of socialism is all right? The Liberal tries to put forward the premise that law enforcement, our local fire department, sewage, etc. is socialism . . . . Hogwash. These are programs of local government that are geared to protect the health and property of the individual. A person who holds to the premise that a police force is socialism doesn't understand the word "socialism." Socialism means government ownership, direction, control and statism, as opposed to individual will. The police are people (a group of individuals) who are hired by the community to protect us from those who assault our private property. When people directly or indirectly authorize government to take from some and give to others, then they have socialism.

Look for the false premise . . . . it is there in practically all of the socialist clichés.

CHAPTER XVI

THE COMMON DENOMINATOR
or
OX GORING

A few years ago I was lecturing to a group about the evils of Socialism. I could tell I had a sympathetic audience .... they remained awake; that is, with the exception of one kind soul. His head kept falling forward, and I am sure he would have started snoring if it hadn't been for his wife's sharp elbow constantly jabbing into his side.

Surely he was attending under duress. He obviously didn't care much for what I was saying, or else he didn't understand. It could have been both.

Later, I changed my tactics and started commenting on taxes. I quoted one fact about how many taxes were in a single loaf of bread, and suddenly my sleepy friend snapped to attention and hung breathlessly upon my every word.

Somehow I had "gored his ox."

Later, after the audience had departed, I asked the hostess, "Who was that fellow in the corner?"

"Oh," she replied, "he's my next door neighbor. His wife's okay, but he's been a tough one to talk to."

"I really got to him on the loaf of bread taxes."

"No doubt," she said, "he's got eight kids and the local bakery truck is by his house twice a day."

With that gentleman I had found a "common denominator." We both disliked hidden taxes, especially when they are wrapped in cellophane.

The way to find the common denominator is through questioning the person to whom you're speaking. Sometimes Conservatives try to cover a multitude of subjects, seeking to find something that will interest the other person. This can more often work against you than for you, because if not handled properly, you wind up in a heated debate long before you stumble across something on which you both agree.

Probe . . . . Ask questions. Ask his advice or opinion. Try not to commit yourself until you find a common denominator.

How often have you heard a fellow Conservative bending some uninformed housewife's ear on the fiscal irresponsibility of our monetary policy? The poor housewife couldn't even contemplate, much less discuss intelligently, the fiscal irresponsibility of the monetary system because she has no understanding of the subject. Talk to her about Johnny's education, or lack of it, and you probably will have a tuned-in audience.

Each person has to relate himself to the subject matter. We sometimes get so "fact and figure" conscious that we overlook the necessity of matching our message to our audience.

It was once said 50,000,000 deaths by Communist hands is a statistic; a child being killed by a car on your block is a tragedy. The truth is they are both tragedies.

You can talk about the many American deaths in Vietnam and that is a statistic, but if you say that Lt. Alvarez was dragged down a filthy North Vietnamese street by the Viet Cong and spat upon (which he was) and add that he could have been the next-door neighbor's boy, then that means something.

The better you develop the ability to paint verbal pictures which people can see and identify, the better you communicate. Your ability to emotionally involve a person in the conversation has a great deal to do with whether he retains what is said.

Remember this. Emotions play a large part in getting a person active in the anti-Communist, anti-Socialist fight. Emotional involvement is not a sin. It can be harmful only when it clouds reason.

I get emotionally upset when I think of the crimes being perpetrated against humanity by the Communists, or any totalitarian system. I would be less than human if I didn't; but if I allowed my emotions to rule me, I would lose my ability to reasonably approach others.

It is characteristic of Conservatives to build their emotions upon facts while Liberals build their "facts" upon emotions.

Our national bureaucracy has become so large that Americans have a difficult time personally relating to it or understanding its machinations. Yesterday's millions are today's billions. Millions, billions, or trillions for that matter are just statistics which people have become accustomed to.

The Conservative says: "We're billions and billions in debt."

"So what?" says his Fuzzy friend to himself. "I'm living fine. I've heard that gripe before. That's just Conservative propaganda."

It is obvious that our Fuzzy friend has no idea how the debt relates to him and what it will mean to the children. If he did, he wouldn't say, "So what?"

Ask your friend if he would go shopping, buy something worth thousands of dollars for his personal use and charge it to his children's account, knowing full well that they would be expected to pay it off when they came of age?

No thinking parent would do that intentionally.

Then point out that this is exactly what we are doing by allowing the government to go deeper into debt.

Our task is to do a better job of relating our subjects to our friends so they will understand. When you graphically show people how much one billion dollars is and how much in hock their kids are, a billion then, and only then, means something.

Find out how you "gore" the interest of your friend.

Sometimes (pardon the pun), all you have to do is "ox" him.

CHAPTER XVII

RECAPTURE OUR WORDS

I started to call this chapter "Use Their Words," but that wouldn't be true. It is more fitting to say "recapture ours," reclaim what once was our property.

The "left" has associated itself with some pretty fine words which invoke happy thoughts in many people. The left shudders when we use these words properly. I have seen Socialists wail like banshees when a true Liberal calls himself liberal.

We Conservatives sometimes react against good words because we associate them with the left.

For example, take the term "Civil Rights!" A civil right is a right protected by law. We are the

91

defenders of a country ruled by law. Why should we allow those who claim to be for civil rights, and then break civil law in the process, call themselves "defenders of civil rights?"

So, used properly, we're for civil rights.

We are all for social justice and progress. We're for equality under law (obviously, since we're Constitutionalists). We're for the brotherhood of man and we are the true protectors of human dignity.

We believe in human rights. What is more a human right than the right to own or dispose of the fruits of one's own labor?

I might add, I'm for the Great Society. Our forefathers conceived it, brought human dignity to man by having faith in his ability, left him alone, and created a great society of individuals.

I am also for a "war on poverty." I am for more jobs being created though a free system, unburdened with bureaucrats.

If you want to see your Left-wing friends come totally unglued, start using these terms in your conversations. They will sputter, stammer and become quite confused.

We should also use words which denote force and violence, and use them in their proper context.

Communism is Red Fascism, totalitarianism, bigoted and extreme, warmongering, hate mongering, corrupt, and ultra reactionary.

The Welfare State and Socialism are the breeding grounds for Nazism, pure and simple. Hitler rose to power in a National Socialist movement. The paper-hanger was a first-class Socialist.

A government official who controls and manipulates news could be called a Hitlerite or Himmlerite. That's what the Nazis did, control news.

A "Hate-peddler" or "Hate-monger" is anyone who tries to breed contempt and hate between races, and many of the "civil rights" groups are perfect examples of this phenomenon. In fact, there is strong evidence to support the claim that creating hatred between Americans of all colors is their prime function. Ask yourself, is there more understanding now between races, or more hatred?

Words are weapons capable of striking blows for truth and understanding, or capable of evoking uncontrolled and controlled reactions which sometimes lead to the destruction of man's higher aspirations.

As I said before, use words . . . . *don't let them use you!*

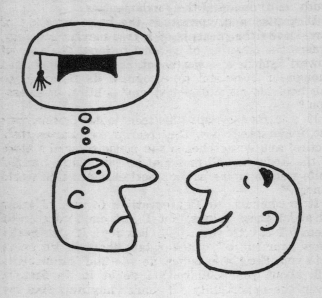

CHAPTER XVIII

KNOW YOUR SUBJECTS

It goes without saying that you should know something about a subject before you start talking. If you are ignorant on a particular matter, at least you can keep people wondering about your knowledge if you keep quiet. Unfortunately, all too often people open their mouths and remove all doubt.

Many Conservatives believe they should know all about every facet of Socialism and Communism before they speak up against it. They feel they should know all the ins-and-outs, facts and figures, on Free Enterprise before they defend it. These people are wrong, because it is impossible for anyone to know ALL the facts. (This might come as a shock to some political southpaws, but it is true).

One thing anybody can do, by hard work and study, is understand the fundamentals.

If a person comprehends the basic function of law, knows the precepts of a free market economy, grasps the meaning of a Constitutional "balance of power" system of government, and then has studied enough of Socialism to recognize its fallacies, he can hold his own in almost any political conversation.[15]

If a person grasps the techniques Communists use, understands how they recruit, recognizes their tactics, and comprehends the conspiratorial nature of the Reds, he will find that he can handle himself quite well in conversations pertaining to this world cancer.[16]

It is common for Conservatives to say, "I know all about these things, but I just can't talk about them." I say to you . . . . boloney! If you really know your subject, you can talk about it. I'll prove it to you. First, you ladies, do you find it difficult to talk about your children? I doubt it. In fact, if given the opportunity (if you're anything like my wife), you will go on for hours about their good habits, future, school, etc. You can talk about your children because you KNOW them.

Now you gentlemen, I'll bet you could talk for hours about your business, favorite sport, your children's future, etc. You know and like the subject; that's why you can converse on the matter.

You can know and talk about Conservatism the same way if you take time to study and know your subject. There is a difference between studying a subject and knowing it!

Knowledge is good only as it is applied. The Communists, as an example, couldn't care less how much you study them, just as long as you don't take your knowledge and do anything with it. I know quite a few people who "study" Communism religiously. *If the Communists ever take this country, these*

*students will know exactly how it was done . . . .
big deal!*

That is small comfort to them, or to you and me.
I say again . . . . use your knowledge. What good is
it if it isn't applied?

First of all, let's remember what we read. Unfortunately, the older we get the sloppier our reading habits tend to become. We subconsciously have
a tendency to read for the emotional effect we receive from the book. We seldom consciously read a
book to retain and pass on information.

How many times have you finished reading a
book, and when asked, "How was it?"

     You replied, "It was great!"

     "What did it say?"

     "It said we were in awful trouble!"

     "What trouble?"

     "Oh, lots of trouble!"

     "Where are we having this trouble?"

     "Everywhere!"

     "How come?"

     "Don't ask me, read it for yourself!"

The person in question had read emotionally, not
retentively.

How many times have you heard a good lecturer
speak for two hours, and afterwards find you can't
remember or repeat five minutes of what the speaker
said? If this is the case, my friend, you read or
listen emotionally.

It wasn't always this way. When you were in
school you remembered what you read. You made
a habit of remembering. Why? Because there was
always some teacher around who had a habit of
giving tests. We sometimes lose good habits that
we have developed. Remembering subject matter is
one of them. It is a habit that we have to develop
again if we hope to convince others of the soundness
of our position.

There are several techniques that are valuable
reading tools. They will help you immeasurably if
you use them.

One technique is paper strips. This is my personal favorite. Take fairly large strips of paper and inset one every third page. When you come to the strip of paper, close the book and try to conscientiously remember what you have just read. Probably you will be surprised how seldom you even remember the last paragraph. Then skim over what you have just read and watch it all come back to you. Then ask yourself, "How can I use that information in a conversation?" If you do this, you will be surprised how much you will retain.

It is better to read one book well and retain its message than read ten books and be unable to communicate on any of them. A book can be a wonderful tool. Between its covers, the author shares years of accumulated knowledge, hoping that it will benefit you.

Second technique . . . . the old underlining pencil. Sometimes use different colored pencils; red for real hot stuff, blue for secondary information, green for other paragraphs that you want to remember. I believe research books should be extensively marked. We're not in the fight to impress people with how clean and pretty our material looks on a bookshelf.

Third technique: Read the same book three times. I find that going back over books I have read before is tremendously beneficial. I learn and retain almost three times the information the second time around. If you have several books on the same general subject, read them all once and then repeat the readings. This will give you a deeper insight, and enable you to derive even more benefit from subsequent readings.

Fourth technique: Form a discussion group with friends on books, and write a short, simple outline on each chapter. This technique is a beauty. You share your knowledge with others and in return gain knowledge from them. Talking about a book and writing a simple outline implant knowledge firmly in your mind.

There are many other valuable techniques which help. It isn't important what method you choose, as long as you retain and then use the material you read.

If you have sloppy reading habits, correct them.

CHAPTER XIX

THE GREATEST WEAPON

Many years ago I was asked to speak before a service club. It wasn't a typical speaking engagement . . . . it was special. A few weeks prior to this talk, my political opponent had spoken to my service club, and now under duress, his service club was returning the favor.

The meeting was held above a bar, in a dark, poorly ventilated room. The atmosphere left a great deal to be desired; in fact, it was gruesome. It was obvious that they had strong pre-conceived ideas on what kind of a person I was. In their minds, I was "their boy's" opponent.

The audience was sparse; many of the members

had stayed home . . . . so I thought. I was to speak on "Captive Nations." I had prepared my notes well in advance, and they were tucked in my inside coat pocket, getting damp from nervous perspiration.

I don't care how many talks a speaker has given . . . . a hostile audience can and does make him very nervous. This time I wasn't just nervous . . . . I was EXTREMELY nervous.

As is the custom, I occupied a seat at the head table. Someone placed the food in front of me, and I commenced to eat. I dislike eating before I speak, but I wasn't going to tip anybody off that I was ill-at-ease; and not eating is an obvious clue to a nervous stomach.

I looked up from my plate and tried to observe the audience . . . . what there was of it. I had the feeling of impending doom when one of them would look at me with a "I know something you don't know" grin, and then look away.

The time for my talk drew near. My mouth had that dry-cotton feeling; my palms were wet with sweat.

My nervousness, in a matter of moments, turned into raw fright . . . . for just as I was about to be introduced, a hoard of people entered the room, filling it to overflowing! In the center of the group was my opponent, surrounded by all of the hard-core lefties in the district! They were laughing and joking. They were there for the hanging . . . . MINE.

My opponent had a chair reserved for him directly in front of the podium. It was all pre-arranged. The goose was about to be cooked, and my opponent was there to watch the plucking.

I wish I could say that my eyes filled with excitement at the challenge that had been presented to me, and that like James Bond 007, I picked up the gauntlet that had been thrown upon the podium, and with complete confidence faced the dawn, firing squad, et al.

But what I would have liked to have been and

what I was were two different things. I was no longer nervous . . . . I WAS PETRIFIED.

My mind was numb. Instead of just having cotton in my mouth, I had the entire cotton belt. I felt it coming out of my ears. My shirt was wet from perspiration . . . . I was a mess!

I heard the club program chairman introduce me and, with no small effort, I stood up and moved toward the podium.

This wasn't JUST a speech. It wasn't JUST a political campaign. My opponent and I were as opposite as night and day. This campaign was to me a moral as well as a political battle. It was serious business.

The distance from my chair to the podium was a little over six feet, the length of a grave. I BOWED MY HEAD AND PRAYED. I asked God for help and asked Him to use me. I took my damp notes out of my pocket and discarded them upon the table. I grabbed the podium in both hands, looked out over the grinning audience without the foggiest idea of what I was about to say. My eyes slowly viewed the crowd, finally resting upon my opponent.

I spoke and was startled by the fact that my voice was sharp and clear, "I see that my opponent is here, and I believe that this is to the advantage of the audience. Instead of just hearing from me, why don't both of us present our views on matters that concern you . . . . the voters?"

My opponent was startled. He hadn't expected this. He tried to decline, but I forced the issue. Finally, he moved around the podium and faced the audience, which was as equally unprepared for this as he.

The first question from the floor was about the Captive Nations . . . . the debate began.

For one complete hour I could do no wrong and he could do no right. He got mad, lost his composure, ranted and raved. He went down in flames in front of his own audience . . . . hoisted by his own petard.

It was a great day!

After it was over, my administrative assistant and I descended the stairway and walked out into the sunshine. He turned to me and said, "Bill, I think God was with you today."

He was right. How did I know? . . . . Simple, I DIDN'T HAVE EITHER THE NERVE OR THE MENTAL AGILITY TO HANDLE MYSELF AS WELL AS I DID. I DON'T HAVE THAT KIND OF STRENGTH. I ASKED FOR AND RECEIVED HELP. I FELT A CONFIDENCE AND STRENGTH THAT I HAD NEVER KNOWN BEFORE.

Ever since that day, before every speech, I ask for His help and ask Him to use me. I never feel alone when I am on a platform.

We have, if we ask for it, the greatest of all strength, the help of the Eternal God.

After all of the study that you and I might do, we usually come to the crux of the matter, which is the fight between good and evil. The power of the Archangel Lucifer against our Saviour Christ.

When we face this Satanic force, we are kidding ourselves if we believe we can lick it alone. We need a greater ally, and we have one. HE'S ALWAYS THERE TO HELP. All we have to do is ask. All He asks of us is to follow.

It is important that we all avail ourselves of His strength. We do that by constant exposure to His word, through the Bible and daily prayer. The best tool of all in bringing people to the truth is by our own personal witness. Let the Eternal God work through you.

We, as Christians, have the greatest weapon!

We, as Christians, have the ultimate victory!

MAN OR MACHINE?

Have you ever looked upon yourself as an accident of nature? In other words, have you ever given much thought to whether you were created by a superior force (God), or that you owe your present existence to a multitude of accidents in nature which took thousands and thousands of years to complete?

Man has and should ponder his origin. Who am I? How did I get here? Where am I going? And, how should I live? Man usually comes to one of two basic conclusions. (1) There is a God and He did create the universe and all that is therein or, (2) there is no God and thus man is nothing but a graduate animal, developed over millions of years through a total evolutionary process, and now owes his existence to accidents which took place within nature.

Our whole Western civilization is built upon the first premise . . . . that man is created; he has a Creator, and this Creator has established moral laws as well as physical laws, which determine how mankind shall live together.

There are those who accept the premise that man is nothing more than a graduate animal, but in his everyday life, lives by the rules and regulations of civilization. We are at this time not concerned with this kind of atheist.

Then there are the Communists and the one-world Socialists. They believe that man is an animal, a very complex animal. They believe that there are smart animals (that's them), and there are dumb animals (that's us). The Communists believe that we, the dumb animals, who accept a divine Creator, are idol-worshipping slobs.

Lenin, who was the daddy Communist of them all, wrote that "Atheism is an integral part of Marxism. Consequently a class-conscious Marxist party must carry on propaganda in favor of atheism."

Lenin also stated that, *"Religion teaches those who toil in poverty all their lives to be resigned and patient in this world, and consoles them with the hope of reward in heaven. As for those who live upon the labour of others, religion teaches them to be charitable in earthly life, thus providing a cheap justification for their whole exploiting existence and selling them at a reasonable price tickets to heavenly bliss. Religion is the opium of the people.* Religion is a kind of spiritual intoxicant, in which the slaves of capital drown their humanity and their desires for some sort of decent human existence.*[17]

If a person took the time, he could fill a volume

*This aphorism was employed by Marx in his criticism of Hegel's Philosophy of Law. After the October Revolution it was engraved in the walls of the former City Hall in Moscow, opposite the famous shrine of the Iberian Virgin Mother. This shrine has now been removed.

with all the quotes that Socialists and Communists have made attacking all forms of religion.

From these morsels of blasphemy, you probably get the idea, if you didn't already know, that Communists are dyed-in-the-wool atheists. In fact, to be a Communist you HAVE to be an atheist . . . . it's fundamental!

I might add, atheists are not necessarily Communists. In fact some atheists are strongly anti-Communist and anti-Socialist, but you can bet that all Communists are atheists. If they weren't they wouldn't be in the conspiracy. It's one of their basic requirements.

Now we have to ask ourselves . . . . "What does this mean to us?" We know that Communists are atheists. We know they don't believe in God . . . . so what?

Their attitudes mean a great deal to us because their very attitudes towards a God, or a lack of God, affects their actions.

From their viewpoint, man is nothing more than a very complex animal, comparable to an extremely complex machine that walks, talks and sometimes thinks. His opinions, beliefs, and attitudes are totally brought about by the forces of society that surround him . . . . i.e. what he hears, sees, or feels.

The Communists view man's brain as an intricate system of nerve wiring and memory cells; a circulatory mechanism which could be compared to a highly developed computer.

Since man's brain, which directs his actions, is like a computer, it will respond like a computer if scientifically manipulated.

Much of their propaganda warfare is based on this concept. A computer cannot emit any information that first hasn't been scheduled (programmed) into it. A computer can only give data based upon what has been scheduled into its memory cells.

Push a button and out comes specific information. Trigger the machine and answers are given based upon pre-programmed information. Such computers are a form of servo-mechanism. "Servo" means "slave" or slave mechanism. The scientific community has developed these slave mechanisms to speed up our productive forces, and today we have many computers which make business more efficient and effective.

Programming one of these machines is all-important. If incorrect information is fed to (programmed) and stored in the machine's memory cells, naturally any "conclusions" of the machine are erroneous. The people in the computer industry have a name for it, "GIGO," meaning garbage in, garbage out.

The Communist looks upon man as a slave mechanism. Like his computer counterpart, he is to be studied and information is to be stored (programmed) in him, in the same manner as you would program a computer.

The conspiracy is doing just that, and quite effectively I might add. The Communists believe that it is the State's function to control the programming of its subjects. They, the Communists, believe that man can be programmed to like or dislike, hate or love, be passive or violent. In a word, man can be made a "servo" for the State, and what's more, like it.

The London Times, May 16, 1956, reported on how the Chinese Reds moulded the mind of a small Chinese businessman, and made him like it. ". . . . *he saw which way things were going and he went along to the authorities to present them with his concern.*

"Instead of thanking him for his generous and forward-looking offer, they chastised him pretty severely, told him that they were not at all satisfied that his offer was made of his own spontaneous will without ulterior motives, and sent him back to think it quietly over by himself. They would not interfere, they said; they wanted only willing and convinced volunteers. Back he went at the end of the month; back he was sent again to search his heart. Then,

when he naturally pressed his offer still more fervently with each delay, and when they finally agreed that his motives were pure, they reminded him of his shareholders. Were they all of one heart and voice? He had to call a meeting of the group, and only then—when they were all clamoring to be allowed to tread the new way—only then did the state agree to take over the concern from them, promising them a share in the profits."[18]

It is interesting today in America how many businessmen are clamoring to the government for subsidies, contracts, advice and help, and how the state is promising them a share in the profits.

Back to China and the Times article, *"It was a glimpse into the process of "moral regeneration" or "brainwashing," about which so much is heard in China. It cannot be left out in any attempt to understand the forces at work . . . . nothing is more striking than the skill and patience with which party members all down the line work on people's minds. Supported by all the social pressures, they spend hours, days and weeks in striving for conversion and willing cooperation wherever possible. And they get results, whether in public confession or private avowals. Where Russia set out to shape lives first and foremost, China is embarked on the task of shaping minds as well."*[19]

In this grand plan for man, the Communists have a growing problem. They call it the counter-revolutionary mentality . . . . that's us.

Because we are not "enlightened" to the make-up of man, and for some archaic reason believe man is more than a product of his environment, we stand as an ever-present danger to the grand new order. We are diseased people as far as they are concerned. We are infecting the world with our counter-revolutionary thinking. We offer to the world conflicting propaganda. So obviously we must be cut out of the world's political body like a surgeon would remove a cancer.

Individuals, groups, and whole nations CAN and

ARE being programmed by Communist propaganda to accept dogmas which are alien to their own survival.

It is possible that by both omission and commission, a substantial percentage of Americans are being fed CONTROLLED information so that they react almost upon command. "Cybernetics" and "servomechanisms" are important sciences when used by those who wish to control the world. They are sciences of which we must be aware. People can be conditioned or programmed. Information can be stored within an individual by design. People do act upon or react to specific stored information. Social environment, to a degree does affect man's outlook. He is affected by the information forces that surround him. MANY TIMES LIKE A COMPUTER, MAN WILL REACT IN A PRE-DETERMINED MANNER BASED UPON HIS PRIOR CONDITIONING OR PROGRAMMING.

To believe that man can be *totally* controlled and to deny that man cannot, of his own accord, rise above or control his thought processes, is fallacious, but at the same time to deny that man cannot be scientifically programmed to think in a specific direction for a period of time is also incorrect. Abe Lincoln said it when he stated, "You can fool all of the people some of the time, some of the people all of the time, but you can't fool all of the people all of the time."

By this time you are probably wondering what all of this has to do with winning arguments with your friends. It is vital!

We, because of our nature, background and moral training, are generally very predictable in any given argument. The Socialist and Communist have recognized our habits, and have systematically conditioned people to react against us and our arguments. Through conditioning, they have made black white, and truth falsehood; they have made individualism look selfish, and have portrayed Conservatism as a dirty word. With their ability to predict our reactions in advance, they have pre-conditioned people to reject us as the bad guys.

As an example: The American people have been sold a big bill of goods on the United Nations being the greatest thing since sliced bread, but the Communists haven't stopped with just pointing out what they consider to be the most salable points of their "Babel by the East River." They knew that in time people would start questioning the effectiveness of this "instrument of peace." They started systematically to discredit through name-calling, innuendo and outright lies, all who might oppose the U.N. They portrayed the U.N. as above reproach and the anti-U.N.'ers as being infidels. So if you speak out against the U.N. in the expected manner, you identify yourself as an "extremist-warmonger" in the minds of most people.

The Communists have pre-conditioned people against an intelligent reaction to the U.N.

Does this mean that you can't argue against the U.N.? . . . . not at all. In fact, knowledge of pre-conditioning gives you an extremely valuable weapon in winning arguments. This was covered in the discussion concerning techniques of persuasion.

If you don't believe in this pre-conditioning . . . . just go out tomorrow and strike up a conversation with a not-too-informed-friend. State that you think the U.N. is a Communist hot-bed, and watch him react against you. Then go to another friend (it is pre-supposed that you still have friends), do the same thing, and watch the identical reaction . . . . "Wats-a-matter . . . . do you want war or sumthin? Don't you wanna talk with other nations? What would you put in its place, wise-guy?" etc., etc.

A conscientious parent doesn't wait until small-pox strikes his child before he does something about it. Wise parents take their children to a doctor and have them inoculated against the disease.

Communists, believing that we are a disease, are constantly inoculating people against our beliefs and principles.

UNNATURAL REACTIONS

If you had a violent fellow in your block who disliked you intensely and made no bones about it, I doubt if you would invite him over to your house to baby-sit with your children.

If this same fellow wrote a book stating clearly that he was going to kill you and your friends, and adding insult to injury, graphically outlined how he was going to do it with your money, you would probably think he was a candidate for the happy farm, straight-jacket and all. But, if you loaned him the money and then stood idly by as he proceeded to systematically carry out his detailed program of shortening your natural life span, you should be proper fodder for a psychiatrist's couch.

The Communists have written volumes of material on how they intend to destroy our Nation, and we don't seem to pay any attention. Simply put . . . . we are "good neighbor Sam" lending our loot to "Ivan the terrible neighbor."

For this country it's unnatural. It is not natural for any individual or nation to lend its enemy money, buy him arms, train his troops and feed him, and at the same time disarm. I say again . . . . it's unnatural.

How many of you have conscientiously planned long-range insurance programs to protect you in your old age, send your children through college, or protect your family from harm? How is it that Americans can look into the future in this manner, but at the same time be totally oblivious to totalitarian forces which are intent on destroying all of our future plans?

You don't build a new wing on your home when the garage is on fire!

Pavlov, in his experiments with animals (and later with people) discovered that the dogs could be conditioned to act unnaturally. A dog normally doesn't salivate when he sees an empty bowl of food. Man normally does not disarm himself in the face of an ever-present danger.

The Communists are systematically trying to condition the American people to act unnaturally. Through the use of emotional tensions, threat of war and nuclear holocaust, offering of peace, racial riots, etc., the Communists bring about stresses upon the emotions of the American people. If these stresses can be applied repeatedly, deep anxieties are generated.

Dr. William Sargant, author of "Battle For The Mind," stated: *Once a state of hysteria has been induced in men or dogs by mounting stresses which the brain can no longer tolerate, protective inhibition is likely to supervene. This will disturb the individual's ordinary conditioned behavior patterns. In human beings, states of greatly increased suggestibility are also found; and so are their opposites, namely, states in which the patient is deaf to all suggestions, however sensible."*[20]

In other words, confuse people, create anxieties, and then when the people are in a state of mental turmoil, suggest to them solutions which on the surface sound plausible, but underneath are totally opposite to normal behavior patterns.

Professor Sargant, commenting on the English people's susceptibility to propaganda during the Second World War: *". . . . hysteria was also evidenced in the susceptibility to rumors of Londoners during the blitz. Brain exhaustion led them to believe stories about 'Lord Haw-Haw's' broadcasts from Germany which they would have at once rejected as untrue when in a more relaxed and less exhausted state. The anxiety engendered by the fall of France, the Battle of Britain, and the blitz created a state in which large groups of persons were temporarily conditioned to accept new and strange beliefs without criticism."*[21]

The fall of Cuba, only ninety miles away from our shores; South Vietnam, where Americans are dying; Laos; the Congo; student riots; race demonstrations, and so forth, literally bring about in Americans the anxiety and confusion necessary to make them receptive to controlled programmed suggestions which are contrary to their basic nature. As an example, we send aid to Communist countries while Americans die from Communist bullets in South Vietnam. If that isn't unnatural, I would like to know what is.

You may wonder what this has to do with talking to your friends about world problems. It has everything to do with it. The more aware you are of how people are affected by systematic conditioning processes, the more effective you will be in communicating. This knowledge allows you to better understand your friends. The whole conspiracy is competing for people's minds, so the more you know of the enemy's tactics, the better equipped you are.

If you are aware of how your friends will react under given circumstances, you have a definite advantage in conversations.

By now you might be saying: "That might be true for others, but no one could brainwash me. That just doesn't happen to good ole normal Americans like me."

May I quote from Professor Sargant again: *"It is a popular fallacy that the average person is more likely to resist modern brainwashing techniques than the abnormal. If the ordinary human brain had not possessed a special capacity of adaptation to an ever-changing environment—building up ever-changing conditioned reflexes and patterns of responses, and submitting for the time being when further resistance seemed useless—mankind would never have survived to become the dominant mammal."*[22]

Professor Sargant then goes on to say: *"That among the readiest victims of brainwashing are the simple, healthy extrovert."*[23]

Aldous Huxley spoke of the effect of mass conditioning in a special appendix to his, "Devils of Loudun." He stated: *". . . . new and previously undreamed-of devices for exciting mobs have been invented. There is the radio, which has enormously extended the range of the demagogue's raucous yelling. There is the loud-speaker, amplifying and indefinitely reduplicating the heady music of class hatred and militant nationalism. There is the camera (of which it was once naively said that 'it cannot lie') and its off-spring, the movies and television. . . . Assemble a mob of men and women previously conditioned by a daily reading of newspapers; treat them to amplified band music, bright lights, and the oratory of a demagogue who (as demagogues always are) is simultaneously the exploiter and the victim of herd intoxication, and in next to no time you can reduce them to a state of almost mindless subhumanity. Never before have so few been in a position to make fools, maniacs or criminals of so many.*"[24]

"Watusi, anyone?"

Dr. Sargant in "Battle For The Mind" states: *"Despite the success of such assaults on the emotions, Western democracies underestimate their political importance . . . ."* and *"It is still considered a mystery how Hitler persuaded even many intelligent people in Germany to regard him as little short of a god; yet Hitler never concealed his methods, which included deliberately producing such phenomena by organized excitement and mass hypnotism, and even boasted how easy it was to impose 'the lie of genius' on his victims. The strength of the Mau Mau rebellion was underestimated by the Kenya authorities who did not realize that Jomo Kenyatta, the originator, never appealed primarily to the intellect of his followers; instead he deliberately used an emotional religious technique for political purposes."*[25]

Most of you are probably aware of Kenyatta's Communist background and his eventual take-over of the Kenya government. He is now one of the "respected" leaders of the "newly emerged nations."

Hitler and Himmler were pikers in comparison with the Communist in techniques of propaganda. They were the kindergarten variety compared to the Communists.

Normal people can be receptive to propaganda. If any of our readers believe that they can't be influenced or duped at one time or another by Communist propaganda, then they are fooling nobody but themselves.

(For further details on propaganda analysis see Appendix III.)

MOTIVATIONAL RESEARCH

If known research techniques are available, they should be used. These methods are available. Properly conducted Motivational Research can accurately tell a businessman what people think of his product, and what people want to see changed.

Properly conducted Motivational Research can tell what issues are important to the voter, and accurately determine how the candidate can best present his principles and program.

Conservatives have a tendency to reject polls. The Conservative generally believes that polls are used as vehicles for propagandizing. Occasionally certain polls are used for this purpose. Public opinion can be molded by polls. No one who has studied communications can deny that. But if the Conservative believes that an accurate poll (Motivational Research) cannot be inaugurated to gain specific knowledge, then he is sadly mistaken.

Motivational Research properly conducted is a valuable tool, a tool that the Conservative usually knows nothing about, or one that he discounts as insignificant.

Motivational Research is an important tool of the left-wing in this country, and I believe an extremely valuable tool to the Communists.

In preceding chapters we talked about the programming of information within the individual, the storing of emotions and information. Motivational Research is the vehicle used to test the effectiveness of this programming. This is called the feed-back factor; or in motivational research, feed back information which can be computed to tell the effectiveness of the program. Motivational Research can tell to a high degree of accuracy what has happened, what is happening, and under controlled conditions, what will happen.

It is important to explain how Motivational Research works. Let's use a specific example. In 1962 I ran for the United States Congress. The State of California was reapportioned (better known as gerrymandered) and new districts were created. One of them was the "29th District." I won the Primary in this district.

A few of us in the campaign were extremely concerned about the voting habits of the people in the 29th District, and so we called in a top Motivational Research organization. They did a very comprehensive and accurate job.

First they ascertained what specific information would be required, such as what were the most important issues affecting the district; if the public knew who the candidates were; what the voters thought of the candidates; what publications they read; what the voters thought of government and many other issues.

We wanted to know in what direction our campaign should go; what obstacles we had to overcome, how deep were party loyalties, in what publications we should place our ads and what were our chances of victory.

The Motivational Research organization first took advantage of existing facts from the Bureau of Statistics and other reputable research organizations. This information allowed our research firm to establish the criteria for selection. These statistics established voter registration, income, church affiliation, size of family, age category, ethnic background, etc.

The sample survey was conducted in selected precincts. Approximately 800 interviews were distributed proportionately throughout the district. All the interviews were made in the home. The selection of male and female respondents was carefully controlled to insure proper division by sex.

Professionals in Motivational Research made the first contacts in the district, and asked the questions which were carefully worded and geared to elicit specific information.

By the process of scientific elimination, they were able to sift through the interviews and isolate families which represented the average voter in the district. When that was accomplished, the staff sent trained psychologists (holding one or more degrees) into these selected homes for "depth" interviews. People were asked indirect questions over a three to four hour period. These questions were designed to seek out their true feelings.

After the second phase was accomplished, the information was fed through the computer and processed. We were then able to establish the percentages of voter reaction on many issues.

The registration of the district was heavily in favor of my opponent from the beginning. It was over two to one. The survey allowed us to establish the various kinds of Republicans and Democrats we were dealing with. The survey was extremely accurate. From it we could predict the outcome of the election months in advance if all the factors remained constant. We knew what areas we had to work in and what we had to do. We cut heavily into my opponent's vote. The final outcome of the election fully substantiated the accuracy of the survey.

The important point is this . . . . properly conducted motivational surveys are quite accurate. You can sift, sort and find key families which are representative of mass thought, and through depth surveys establish what a large percentage of the population is thinking on given subjects.

In the State of California, with the largest state population in America, CBS needed only sixty key precincts to accurately establish and predict the voting patterns of the entire state in the 1964 Presidential election.

Motivational Research is used extensively by the leftists. They test the public before they implement important programs. They certainly don't want a reaction which could hurt their cause.

At one time I wondered how it was possible for the Communists to set up a base ninety miles from our shores and get away with it. I thought that the American people would rise up as one to expel this menace to our hemisphere.

But they did not . . . . why? The reason is simple. The Communists knew in ADVANCE that they could get away with it . . . . and they did. Based upon projected Motivational Research reaction patterns, the facility to control certain facets of communications, coupled with their ability to confuse the issue sufficiently to cause indecision, the Communists set up headquarters on our door-step.

Conservatives should know as much as possible about Motivational Research and how it works. We, too, can use it effectively. It is a tool that is readily available . . . . all we have to do is recognize its significance and use it!

It is fine to be Conservative when it comes to conserving principles and ideas, but if we are Conservative to the degree that we fail to use modern effective methods, we are making a grave mistake.

Motivational Research, contemporary advertising techniques, contemporary graphics, and proper public relations are relatively new. Each one of these fields has developed immensely over the last thirty years.

Our opposition recognizes the potential of these fields and uses them effectively . . . . so should we.

Again I repeat, don't be like certain Conservatives who say: "Well, if *they* use these techniques, then we certainly SHOULDN'T! . . . I would never do that!" Don't confuse TECHNIQUES with PRINCIPLES; to do so is rank stupidity.

A tool is a tool. It all depends no how you use it. The Communists use these tools for evil purposes. We can use them for good.

As regular as clock work, some major Communist thrust will hit the headlines. We will be shocked because the Communist move (or our Government's reaction) creates hardly a ripple in public opinion.

"Why can't people see what's going on? . . . If anything should shake up Americans *that* should," we cry!

But it doesn't . . . . why?

I CONTEND THAT THROUGH A CONTINUING MOTIVATIONAL RESEARCH PROGRAM, THE HIERARCHY OF THE COMMUNIST MOVEMENT KEEPS ITS FINGER ON THE PULSE OF PUBLIC OPINION AND KNOWS IN ADVANCE HOW THE POPULATION WILL REACT.

EPILOGUE

You can be a more effective spokesman for our Nation if you *really* wish to be. Anything that is worthwhile takes time and patience, and contrary to some doom peddlers, I believe we have the time to shape up this Nation if we keep trying.

Totalitarianism is only inevitable when people accept the premise that it is inevitable. You, the reader (yes I mean you) have the responsibility to do something about it. If you don't like what's going on, stop griping and get active. There are hundreds of things that can be done. The first is to educate yourself properly . . . . then develop the facility to communicate your knowledge.

One rapid way to develop the ability to communicate your ideas is to secure a good friend, who is also a Conservative, and practice on each other. One of you should play the part of the "Liberal" and the other the "Conservative," then alternate. When you make a mistake, stop the discussion and analyze. You will be surprised how quickly you will develop good discussion habits. Also, you won't be alienating people while you learn.

One day you will find yourself in a conversation with a strong Liberal friend who formerly verbally boxed you around at will. This time, if you have developed good discussion techniques, you will find that he isn't as glib as you had thought.

He, for a change, is defending, and you are getting your points over, one after another. You will never forget this day . . . . it will be a vintage day! You will find then that you will have more confidence in your ability to talk conservatism, and before long you will be confident enough to discuss your ideas with anyone.

"So you're a Liberal, ADA, ACLU, NAACP, FPA, CORE member, well, well, well. There's a question that I would like to ask you, and if you can keep to the subject we can, etc., etc., etc."

THE END

REFERENCES

1. Hunter, Edward, "Communist Psychological Warfare (Brainwashing);" House Committee on Un-American Activities; U. S. Government Printing Office, Washington, Mar. 13, 1958, p. 12.

2. Ibid. pp. 12 & 13.

3. Edwards, Willard, "JFK's Deceptive Manipulating of the Press;" Human Events, 410 First St. S. E., Washington, D. C.; Feb. 16, 1963.

4. Ibid.

5. Possony, Dr. Stefan T., "Language As A Communist Weapon;" House Committee on Un-American Activities; U. S. Government Printing Office, Washington, Mar. 2, 1959, p. 3.

6. Ibid. p. 1.

7. Ibid. pp. 8 & 9.

8. Ibid. pp. 8 & 9.

9. "New Drive Against the Anti-Communist Program;" Senate Internal Security Subcommittee; U. S. Government Printing Office, Washington, D. C.; 1961.

10. "Twelfth Report Un-American Activities in California;" Senate Fact Finding Committee; State Printing Office, Sacramento, California, 1963.

11. Bastiat, Frederic, *The Law & Cliches of Socialism;* Constructive Action, Inc.; Whittier, California, 1964.

12. Ibid. pp. 248-250.

13. Morris, Robert, *No Wonder We Are Losing;* The Bookailer, New York, 1958.

14. Stormer, John, *None Dare Call It Treason;* Liberty Bell Press, Florissant, Mo., 1964.

15. Bastiat, Frederic, *The Law & Cliches of Socialism;* Constructive Action, Inc.; Whittier, California, 1964.

16. Hoover, J. Edgar, *Masters of Deceit;* Henry Holt & Co., Inc.; New York, 1958; Skousen, W. Cleon, *The Naked Communist;* The Ensign Publishing Co.; Salt Lake City, Utah, 1958.

17. Lenin, V. I., *Religion;* Little Lenin Library, Volume 7, International Publishers, New York.

18. "Moulding Minds for the New China"; London Times, May 16, 1956.

19. Sargant, William, *Battle for the Mind;* Doubleday & Co., Garden City, N. Y.

20. Ibid. p. 59.

21. Ibid. pp. 59-60.

22. Ibid. p. 81.

23. Ibid. p. 81.

24. Ibid. pp. 158-9.

25. Ibid. p. 159.

CONSTRUCTIVE ACTION, INC.
ACTION PROGRAMS

This book is being published at a crucial moment in history. The great world struggle of mind and soul, of life and death is rapidly coming to its climactic crisis in the United States—the last hope of the free world. Will we slide into complete Socialism? (See James Burnham's SUICIDE OF THE WEST.) Or, will enough Americans awaken to the danger and act resolutely to regain freedom? The answer is up to YOU!

The first step is a thorough grounding in the basic principles of our individual freedom under law. The fundamentals of liberty as so clearly presented in the book THE LAW AND CLICHES OF SOCIALISM published by Constructive Action, Inc., give an excellent start toward the necessary "thorough grounding."

Another essential book is NONE DARE CALL IT TREASON by John Stormer. This is a brilliant presentation of the ideological and political problems of today.

SLIGHTLY TO THE RIGHT, is published with the expectation that it will help to make successful communicators of those who have already obtained a thorough grounding in the ideological and political problems of today and the basic principles of individual freedom under law.

Continuing programs of study, self-improvement and action to create widespread knowledge and interest are needed. Constructive Action, Inc. provides such programs. At the present time these include:

1. LOBBY AND RECEPTION ROOM LITERATURE

The reception room or lobby provides an ideal location to bring our citizens into contact with publications giving basic truths and clear explanations of the positive values of Freedom and the Private Enterprise System. Constructive Action, Inc. suggests that the reception room or lobby be supplied with a cross-section of the best magazines, books, newsletters, and pamphlets carrying the message of individual freedom and responsibility. A list of recommended periodicals is shown on page 126. A lending library of basic books and a selection of "take home" pamphlets can be purchased from Constructive Action, Inc.

2. STUDY GROUP MATERIAL—FOR CHURCHES, DORMITORIES, CLUBS, FRATERNITIES, SORORITIES AND OTHERS

These selections of periodicals, manuals, study guides and booklets are designed to provide study material which will promote intelligent discussion and understanding of current events within the framework of Private Enterprise Capitalism and Constitutional Government. They are a MUST for any serious student or study group of current world and national events.

3. BOOK SELECTIONS FOR LIBRARIES

Constructive Action, Inc. offers a selection of books which can be purchased for a personal library or donated for use in public libraries, churches, schools, colleges, fraternities, dormitories, ships, clubs, offices, sororities, or homes.

4. MASSIVE LOW-COST BOOK DISTRIBUTION

Constructive Action, Inc. stocks and sells large quantities of books which have a wide appeal. Low cost distribution is possible because of sales in carton lots. Inventories of these special books are maintained in Chicago, Illinois and Whittier, California.

For detailed information on any of these programs, contact:

CONSTRUCTIVE ACTION, INC.
P. O. Box 4006
Whittier, California 90607
Telephone: Area Code 213-693-0764

WHAT CAN YOU DO?

BECOME INFORMED!

Listen to these Radio and Television Broadcasts:

Life Line   The Manion Forum
The Dan Smoot Report   Fulton Lewis, Jr.

Subscribe to and read these publications:

MAGAZINES

The Freeman   U.S. News and World Report
The New Guard   National Review

NEWSLETTERS

America's Future   Freedom's Facts
Fulton Lewis Reports   The Dan Smoot Report
Life Lines   The Manion Forum

NEWSPAPERS

Human Events   The Freedom Press
Christian Economics   The Wanderer

Join A Study Group (This is MOST Important)

READ Basic Books
See item 3 on page 124. For the latest good books, join
the Conservative Book Club, 542 Main Street, New
Rochelle, New York.

LEARN How Your Political Party Operates.

TAKE EFFECTIVE ACTION!

SUBSCRIBE to and promote Constructive Action's services:
   STUDY GROUP
   LIBRARY
   BOOK DISTRIBUTION

WRITE Letters to:
   Your Senators and Congressman (Federal and State)
   Local, State, and Federal Officials
   The Editors of Your Local Newspapers

WHEN YOU HAVE READ A PUBLICATION, PASS IT ON TO A FRIEND OR LEAVE IT IN A PUBLIC PLACE.

BECOME ACTIVE IN YOUR POLITICAL PARTY.

JOIN A POLITICAL ACTION GROUP TO HELP NOMINATE AND ELECT QUALIFIED CANDIDATES.

For more information about any of these items, contact:

CONSTRUCTIVE ACTION, INC.
P. O. Box 4006
Whittier, California 90607
Area code 213-693-0764